BEATING THE

DOW

WITH BONDS

BEATING THE

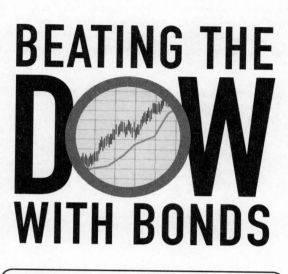

D○W

WITH BONDS

Michael B. O'Higgins
with John McCarty

A High-Return, Low-Risk Strategy

for Outperforming the Pros

Even When Stocks Go South

HarperBusiness
A Division of HarperCollins*Publishers*

BEATING THE DOW WITH BONDS. Copyright © 1999 by Michael B. O'Higgins and John McCarty. All rights reserved. Printed in the United States of America. No part of this book may be used or reproduced in any manner whatsoever without written permission except in the case of brief quotations embodied in critical articles and reviews. For information address HarperCollins Publishers, Inc., 10 East 53rd Street, New York, NY 10022.

HarperCollins books may be purchased for educational, business, or sales promotional use. For information please write: Special Markets Department, Harper-Collins Publishers, Inc., 10 East 53rd Street, New York, NY 10022.

FIRST EDITION

Designed by Ruth Lee

ISBN 0-88730-947-X

99 00 01 02 03 ❖ /RRD 10 9 8 7 6 5 4 3 2

To Donna, my right arm

CONTENTS

ACKNOWLEDGMENTS

I am indebted to many people who have contributed to my investment education over the past thirty years, but I am especially grateful to the following, who contributed directly to the writing and publishing of this book:

John McCarty, my collaborator, without whose talent, imagination, diligent effort, and constant nagging this book would never have been finished on time.

John Rothchild, author of *The Bear Book* (Wiley & Sons, 1998), my good friend and tennis buddy, who reminded me to keep this book simple and unwittingly led me to conceive of it in its present form.

Joseph A. McGraw, owner and founder of Yankee Advisors, who first exposed me to the idea of using the price of gold as a bond market barometer.

Federico Coupe and David Oberting, my loyal, dependable, and talented business associates, for the many hours of tedious statistical research work.

Laureen Rowland, our editor at HarperCollins, who not only appreciated our book idea and sold it to her bosses, but then used her considerable editorial skills to make it better than we could ever have imagined.

Faith Hornby Hamlin, our agent at Sanford J. Greenburger Associates, who brought us together, made us write a super proposal, and got us a great contract.

INTRODUCTION

WILL **R**OGERS **USED** to say that people should be more concerned with the return *of* their principal than the return *on* their principal.

That observation sums up today's out-of-control attitude toward the stock market.

Consider the following:

In July 1996, a federal commission on the long-term future of Social Security, driven by a need for higher returns to meet projected deficits, and to bolster waning public confidence in our nation's principal retirement system, issued recommendations for avoiding the inevitable insolvency of Social Security by the time baby boomers begin retiring in 2010. It took the unprecedented step of proposing that Social Security participants now be empowered to invest a portion of their Social Security contributions in common stocks.

If the Social Security Treasury Fund had invested mostly in the stock market instead of bonds from its inception in the 1930s, there would now be a surplus instead of projected deficits. But the timing for this change in game plan couldn't be more ill advised.

Common stocks are now at their most expensive levels in history—up 98,900 percent since the end of the 1929–1932 Great Crash—and therefore much more susceptible to a decline.

In effect, the commission is closing the barn door after the horses are gone.

Here's another example. In April 1997, the New Jersey State Legislature, anxious to continue the program of yearly tax cuts begun by Governor Christine Todd Whitman in 1995, approved a complicated plan to borrow $3 billion and invest the money in common stocks to cover projected deficits expected as a result of future tax cuts.

The legislature's reasoning? That since the New Jersey Employment Retirement Fund stock portfolio earned an average of 16 percent annually over the last fifteen years, the state could borrow in the bond market at 8 percent and generate $240 million in *new* revenues by earning the difference between its interest expense and what it expected to make in the stock market.

The legislature's reasoning illustrates the cumulative effect of sixty-five years of bull markets. It assumes that the stock market always goes up; a decline simply presents a momentary buying opportunity, a chance to invest more money in the stock market before the next "inevitable" upswing.

This is typical behavior at the end of an upcycle. The legislature is "reaching for yield"*—but the yield it's reaching for isn't there anymore.

One more example. Confidence in the stock market's increasing upward movement has caused more investors to borrow to buy stocks. As evidence, during 1996 more money was invested in U.S. equity mutual funds than was saved in our country. From July 1990 through summer 1997, a period when stocks returned roughly half the 293 percent thrown off in the previous eight years, investors

---

*"Reaching for yield" is a bond market expression describing the tendency of bond investors to invest in lower-grade bonds in the late stages of a rising bond (falling interest rate) market.

poured untold billions into stock mutual funds—90 percent of all the money that has ever been invested in that industry since its inception seventy-plus years ago.

By placing a greater percentage of their wealth at risk than ever before in history, investors are essentially pawning the present for future windfalls. In effect, they are saying, "A bird in the bush is worth two in the hand."

These examples—and I could cite many more—share a common thread. They reflect the widely held assumption that stocks are always the best place to be to make money, that they are a *consistently* profitable investment vehicle. While it is true that over the long term, investing in stocks can be very profitable indeed (see Chapter 4), such an assumption is very ill-founded; it ignores the fact that in the short term, stocks can also be *very risky* (see Chapter 5), something people today have forgotten because the market has been a one-way street for so long.

The truth is that the stock market has declined an average of four out of every ten years in the 116 years since that data first became available in 1881.

In the past thirty-six years alone, there have been eight major stock market declines (see Table 1)—one every four and a half years—lasting an average of almost twelve months and causing the Dow Jones Industrial Average (DJIA) to drop an average of 30 percent.

Table 1
Market Declines Since 1961
Decline Percentage

Period	Duration	Decline
12/31/61–06/26/62	6.4 months	–27.1%
02/09/66–10/07/66	8.0 months	–27.1%
12/03/68–05/26/70	17.8 months	–35.9%
01/11/73–12/26/74	17.2 months	–45.1%
09/21/76–02/28/78	17.2 months	–26.1%

Table 1 (cont.)

Period	Duration	Decline
04/27/81–08/12/82	15.5 months	–24.1%
08/25/87–10/19/87	1.8 months	–36.1%
07/16/90–10/11/90	2.8 months	–21.2%
Average	**11.5 months**	**–30.1%**

And there have been special periods in this century—the afore-mentioned Great Crash of 1929–1932, for example—when stocks have produced *negative returns* for an extended length of time. Sometimes, when such periods occurred, *it took thirty years for investors to get back to even in constant dollars.*

Contrary to popular opinion, stocks are not always the best place to be.

As I've written, they're the best place to be in the long run, but as the upcoming chapters will show, there are definitely periods of time when stocks may not be the most profitable option because the market has become too pricey and/or for other reasons—periods that can sometimes last as long as twenty-five to thirty years. There may be other, better, less expensive and therefore potentially more lucrative options in the short term that investors should give serious consideration to, particularly the U.S. Treasury securities markets. These securities, the only truly low-risk investment vehicles, are reasonably good investments under most economic conditions (depending on their price, of course), but *essential* during bad times when, used in conjunction with stocks, they will lower your level of risk and increase your returns.

What's the Lesson?

After the market has reached extreme valuation levels, stocks have often provided very meager returns or even losses for several decades. This usually causes a vicious chain reaction in which people don't invest, the market declines, more people don't invest, the market declines more, and so on until stocks become so ridiculously cheap that value-oriented investors like me step in to buy and start a new bull market that takes stocks to new highs in real terms some thirty years later. That's an awfully long time for any victim of a down cycle, but especially the average-Joe investor, to break even or see a return.

So, what's the average Joe to do? In a market primarily influenced by psychological factors, I have always believed in doing what other people aren't. When everybody moves to one side of the investment boat, I know it's time to move to the other, not only to keep dry but to keep making money.

Today, as stocks trade at the most expensive levels in history, they are at the low side of the boat in terms of potentially greater reward, because the stock market is where everybody is, pushing prices up and value down.

I believe that the horde of dice-rolling stocks-only investors who have been spoiled by the returns of stocks in the 1990s will, like their counterparts of the 1920s and 1960s, soon regret their ill-timed love affair with stocks, as a lot of them get wet.

This book will show you in a simple and reliable way how to recognize when it's advantageous to be in stocks, when it isn't, where to invest in the short term to perhaps even double your return so that, good times and bad, you'll always stay dry—and keep making money safely, yet very profitably.

PART 1

Introducing T-Bonds, T-Bills, and Stocks

A Strategy for All Seasons

I **BEGAN INVESTING** in the stock market while I was in college.

Being a novice at the game, I subscribed to *Value Line* and a number of other market newsletters for guidance, studied them like crazy, and came to consider myself something of a market wiz—a classic case of a little knowledge being a dangerous thing.

I even tried becoming a stockbroker right after graduating in 1970. But the brokerage industry wasn't interested in me because, contrary to popular belief, stockbrokers are *not* financial consultants. They are securities *salesmen*, and Wall Street doesn't hire people without a track record in sales—that proven ability to stand rejection and keep "smiling and dialing."

So, I got some sales training at Procter and Gamble, and then entered the investment business in 1971, joining Spencer Trask and Company, one of Wall Street's oldest and most prestigious investment research firms, where my job was to sell banks, insurance companies, and other institutional investors our highly regarded research services in return for some of their commission business.

By 1973 to 1974, the market was in the middle of its worst decline in modern times, second only to the Great Crash of

1929–1932. That was when I discovered how worthless traditional investment research truly is, including that of the company for which I worked. Here we were supposed to be the best in the business, yet our clients were losing almost 50 percent of their money following our investment advice!

Like most Wall Street analysts at that time, we were proponents of the strategy of growth stock investing, whereby you identified the best stocks—the so-called Nifty Fifty—and bought them regardless of price. The idea was that no matter how overpriced they were, their projected earnings growth would bail you out.

However, as I researched on my own the various market cycles that have occurred over the years, it struck me that the most important market variable is not earnings growth, but the much harder to predict price to earnings ratio. The P/E ratio is a function of investor *expectations* of future earnings that Wall Street analysts virtually ignore in their projections because, like forecasting what the temperature is going to be a year from now, they are less likely to get it right.

To put this into perspective, the stock market experiences thirteen-year cycles in which earnings either rise or fall dramatically. Historically, during cycles when earnings have exploded upward, stock prices have gone either sideways or down because price to earnings ratios fell enough to offset the effect of any earnings increases.

A perfect example was the 1973–1974 bear market (the last two years of the 1961–1974 cycle), when *earnings* on the DJIA went up 48 percent, while in the face of that increase, the P/E on the DJIA fell from 15.7 to 5.8, causing the *price* of the Dow to decline by 47 percent.

In other words, even though earnings were still coming through, my clients were still getting killed because of the falling price to earnings ratio.

And not only did I find out that Wall Street analysts couldn't predict price to earnings ratios, I began to realize that their earnings predictions weren't red-hot either.

A study I conducted of the accuracy of Wall Street forecasting many years later proves what I mean. I collected ten years of earnings projections by Wall Street analysts from the year-end issue of *Business Week*, and compared the numbers a year later to actual earnings. The average margin of error, up or down, was *54 percent!* In most cases, investors would have done just as well, or poorly, gazing into a crystal ball.

Hunting with the Dow Dogs

Disillusioned with traditional research, I began searching for a better, more reliable method of beating the Dow. One that fit snugly with my contrarian viewpoint that when everyone is placing their bets on the hare, maybe the safer, surer bet is the tortoise. Majority thinking is usually wrong for two reasons. One, consensus in the investment world develops after a trend has been in effect for a long period of time—and the longer such a trend is in effect, the less likely it is to remain that way. Two, usually when there is widespread agreement on a particular investment's attractiveness, it means investors have acted on that opinion, causing the investment's price to move dramatically in one direction. The more expensive an investment gets, the more difficult it is to make money and the riskier it becomes. My rule of thumb: buy cheap, sell dear.

My method also had to be simple—something I would be able to do myself, in my spare time, without having to analyze thousands of companies. This was before the widespread availability of personal computers, when "keeping it simple" was a necessity.

It was a tall order to fill indeed.

But fill it I did—with an Ohio Bank client's "little black box." This was his trust department's "approved" list, a list of the most widely held and popularly followed stocks in the world, around which he had drawn a line in black ink: the thirty blue chip companies making up the Dow Jones Industrial Average (see Table 1.1).

Table 1.1
The Current Dow 30 Industrials

AlliedSignal Inc.

Aluminum Company of America/Alcoa

American Express Company

AT&T Corporation

The Boeing Company

Caterpillar Inc.

Chevron Corporation

The Coca-Cola Company

E.I. du Pont de Nemours and Company

Eastman Kodak Company

Exxon Corporation

General Electric Company

General Motors Corporation

Goodyear Tire & Rubber Company

Hewlett-Packard

International Business Machines Corporation/IBM

International Paper Company

Johnson & Johnson

J.P. Morgan & Co., Inc.

McDonald's Corporation

Merck & Co., Inc.

Minnesota Mining and Manufacturing Company

Philip Morris Companies Inc.

Procter & Gamble Company

Sears, Roebuck & Company

Travelers Group Inc.

Union Carbide Corporation

United Technologies Corporation

Wal-Mart Stores

The Walt Disney Company

These are the market bellwethers, he explained. These companies were of such huge economic importance—due to their large capitalization, history of strong earnings and dividend increases, and ample amounts of cash—that they were likely to do better, longer term than non-Dow companies, largely because of their enormous staying power. Like the proverbial six-hundred-pound gorilla that sits anywhere it wants to, these Dow heavyweights might slip from their desired perch from time to time but they are never away from it for very long.

Something of a maverick in investing circles, he said, "Why not keep it simple and stick with these thirty blue chips rather than follow thousands of publicly traded stocks?"

It made sense because I knew there would always be certain periods when, for one reason or another, some of these Dow stocks would perform well, some would tread water, and some of them would go down.

By investing in a package of five out-of-favor Dow stocks (dividends high, prices low)—the "Dow Dogs," as the financial press has since dubbed them—which no Wall Street analyst would recommend because the outlook for them was generally so "terrible," I found that I could achieve higher, steadier returns at less risk because these companies are major players that seemed always to land on their feet.

Usually, they are number one or two in their respective markets, have a huge infrastructure, a long history, big customer base, and a large revenue stream.

If the problem is poor management, new management comes in, sweeps away past policies, makes strategic changes that adjust to the new realities, kicks the horse's flank to get it moving, and starts making money again.

If the problem is caused by conditions beyond the company's control—a cyclical factor or a temporary financial setback (such as the *Exxon Valdez* oil spill of 1989)—there's not much the company can do except hang in there. But down cycles seldom last, and the

DJIA 30 stocks have the muscle to survive them and recover.

In either case, having bought the stocks cheap, you just sit there getting paid a handsome dividend while you wait for the companies' fortunes to improve and the stocks' prices to ride the up wave again.

This conformed to another investing truism I'd already learned. That in making money, much of the time there is nothing to do. To paraphrase an observation of Warren Buffett, the most successful living, long-term investor: The greatest gains usually come from simply watching your investments grow in value over time.

On my own, I began using my strategy of buying the five cheapest stocks among the ten highest-dividend-yielding stocks on the Dow, and discovered I was outperforming the results of my fellow pros more than 90 percent of the time.

I was beating the Dow by keeping it simple, an approach that is now ingrained.

In fact, as financial markets have now expanded to include virtually every country and an ever-growing number of securities options, the ability of investors and advisors to digest, evaluate, and act on the vast amount of data now available, even with the aid of computers, is still limited.

And so, "keeping it simple" is more a must these days than ever.

My system for beating the Dow worked so well, so consistently, that by 1978 I had enough confidence to take it on the road. I started my own money management firm founded on that system.

When my business succeeded beyond my wildest expectations, I began to feel a desire to write a book and share what I'd learned with the investing public at large.

In an easy-to-understand way, it showed how to use high dividend yields to identify out-of-favor Dow stocks that, as a group, have outperformed the overall Dow average with remarkable consistency, based on the following set of simple principles:

- The key to investment success is knowing value. Buy cheap, sell dear. Get paid in advance by buying undervalued assets.

- By virtue of sheer size and strength—call it raw staying power—the thirty blue chip companies like General Electric and McDonald's that make up the Dow Jones Industrial Average (DJIA) tend to be survivors. The old adage, "the bigger they are, the harder they fall," usually doesn't hold true when you're talking about corporate giants.

- The investing public invariably overreacts to unfavorable developments such as a crisis in the Middle East or a strike by U.S. workers. This creates opportunities when you're dealing with blue chips. With them, bad news is usually good news because it makes strong stocks cheap.

- Recognizing the tendency of less-expensive stocks to move in greater percentage increments than higher-priced shares, my strategy of using the five lowest-priced of the DJIA's ten highest-yielding stocks would identify those stocks whose prices are cheap relative to their current dividends. When held for twelve-month periods, those stocks would produce Dow-beating total returns.

Beating the Dow came out in October 1990. The timing was perfect. We were right at the bottom of the 1990 market collapse. While my strategies had performed well before the book's publication—averaging an annual return of 18.2 percent since I began using them—they did even better afterward, averaging 29.2 percent. As evidenced by the number of people who bought the book and the veritable industry it spawned—including Web sites, mutual funds, and $20 billion worth of investments—it was very satisfying knowing my readers had made a lot of money in such solid blue chips.

A Better Mousetrap

Now, however, compared to conditions that existed when my first book was published—when the DJIA, at 2629, had a P/E of 15 and a dividend yield of 3.95 percent—the DJIA and common stocks in general are at their most overvalued levels ever. Even the so-called cheapest among them (my pet Dow Dogs) are no longer all that cheap anymore. Because of this, it is my belief that today's big bull market is running on fumes, and that the bear may not be clawing at the door yet, but it's sniffing around out in the yard.

Unprepared for the likelihood of a stock market decline as prices inevitably regress to more normal levels, a lot of today's stocks-only investors, many of whom have only an average level of market sophistication and financial strength, may get financially hurt as they scurry to the sidelines to protect what money they have left. Therefore, I felt another, safer and potentially more profitable system with more investment options was needed.

Beating the Dow with Bonds is that system. It doesn't replace my Beating the Dow stock-picking system, which continues to be the championship system for selecting an equity portfolio. But it goes a big step further. It gives you, the average investor, greater flexibility in a changing market by incorporating two more investment choices—U.S. Government Treasury bonds (T-bonds) and Treasury bills (T-bills), and a proven method of determining when it's unsafe to invest in stocks, where to go in the meantime, and when it's safe to get back into stocks again.

With my new system, you'll no longer have to worry about bear markets, and can continue to beat the Dow over longer periods of time with more consistency, lower transaction costs, and much less risk.

In fact, as Chapter 9 will show, my new system would have directed you to stocks in just eight of the past twenty-nine years. In spite of that, you would have done twenty times as well as the Dow 30 and Standard & Poor's 500, almost four times better than you would have done using my stocks-only strategy, and outperformed most money managers.

Why T-bonds and T-bills?

Unlike stocks, T-bonds and T-bills are *undervalued* in relation to their historical levels, and are bargains at this time. Today, while stocks hover around 28.5 times earnings, the most expensive level in history, long-term U.S. T-bonds are paying more than 3 percent real interest. That's more than *double* their historical return, which in the past two hundred years has been lower than today's more than 90 percent of the time.

Let's view it another way.

At 28.5 times earnings, today's stocks-only investor receives an earnings yield of 3.51 percent. The earnings yield is merely the aforementioned price to earnings ratio—in this case 28.5—expressed as a percent.

The same investor might buy ultra-safe 30-year T-bonds yielding 5.8 percent, achieving almost a 68 percent greater return than stocks while bearing only a fraction of the intrinsic risk.

Today's stocks-only investors are banking that their meager 4.00 percent earnings yield will *always* continue to be enhanced by a rising stock market. But what if it isn't? What if, God forbid, the market goes down, as it has 40 percent of the time in this century? What if we have a recession and corporate earnings decline, as they have in twenty-two of the past sixty-seven years? In contrast, T-bonds and T-bills pay a *fixed* rate of interest and *guarantee* the return of your money at a certain date. Moreover, the U.S. government has *never* missed a principal or interest payment or defaulted on its loan obligations—and furthermore, were that unlikely scenario to occur, we'd *all* be passengers on the *Titanic*, and the fate of our earnings would be the least of our worries.

Still Keeping It Simple

For purposes of the average investor, I have sought to keep my new system as simple as my old one. It, too, requires under a half hour of research as seldom as once a year.

Part 1 (Chapters 1–4) and Part 2 (Chapters 5–8) of the book explain the intricacies of the T-bond, T-bill, and stock markets, and the whys of moving your investment portfolio among all three to beat the Dow under all market conditions.

Part 3 (Chapters 9–11) pulls everything together to show you how and when to make your investment choices using my new Beating the Dow with T-bonds, T-bills, and Stocks asset allocation system.

At a fraction of the risk, you will experience less downside volatility (fewer down years) and more upward volatility with my new system. But I don't think making *too much money* will be a major cause of concern or complaint for you.

It's a system that requires a bit more work than my Beating the Dow stocks-only strategy, in that you have to go through several preliminary steps. You will first want to determine whether you want to be in stocks or Treasury Securities. Then, if bonds are indicated, you will decide whether you want to be in T-bonds or T-bills; if stocks are the choice, you will go forward and construct a value-laden portfolio of beaten-down blue chip DJIA components. Yet this system is just as easy to understand and use as its predecessor.

Between now and 2001, as stock valuations and interest rates return to more normal levels, T-bond and T-bill investors should experience very respectable returns while stocks should decline. In the face of that coming stock market decline, average investors like yourself with as little as $5,000 in your pocket to invest will now have more ways to keep beating the Dow while all those stocks-only investors about you are still rolling their dice.

Gentlemen Prefer Bonds

GENTLEWOMEN, TOO—even though in the go-go investment world of the late 1990s, the mere mention of U.S. Treasury bonds, the primary bond instrument of my new Beating the Dow with T-bonds, T-bills, and Stocks strategy, as an attractive option often brings howls of laughter and derision from many quarters.

After all, their prices are lower today than they were four years ago, while stocks have more than doubled. "Don't the 10 percent per annum long-term returns of stocks versus bonds' 5 percent prove the inherent superiority of stocks?" say the conventional thinkers of today. My contrarian answer to that is *no*.

Let's begin by examining the principal—no pun intended—characteristics of bonds in general, T-bonds in particular, and the historical returns of T-bonds under different economic conditions.

What Are Bonds?

In financial market lingo, a bond is a long-term loan made by an individual to an institution, which agrees to repay the full sum of

13

the loan (the principal) at the date of maturity, plus a fixed or floating rate of interest on the money borrowed at established intervals along the way. In other words, it is basically an IOU that promises repayment of your money plus interest over a set period of time.

Though often linked with stocks in the public's mind, bonds are very different. For one thing, the bond market is considerably larger than the stock market in terms of dollars invested. For another, when an individual buys stock, he or she becomes in effect a part owner in the company, sharing in the profits through dividends and retained earnings. Profits, of course, are not assured. They are completely dependent upon how the company's fortunes rise or fall. But when you buy bonds, you become a creditor, owning debt, and you profit from the regular interest payments you receive on the loan until it is paid off.

Although the volume of bonds available to investors is enormous, there are basically only three major types of bonds in the United States: treasuries, corporates, and municipals. Treasuries are issued by the U.S. government, corporates by American companies, and municipals by state and local governments and their agencies. Each issues bonds to raise cash for a wide range of purposes, everything from funding new or existing projects to modernizing and expanding to just plain staying afloat.

Corporations can sell stock to raise capital as well, but often prefer borrowing with bonds—and getting a tax break on the interest paid out—to allowing more fingers into the profit pot by issuing additional stock.

The U.S. Treasury is the largest issuer of such debt in the world, almost 43 percent, most of it since 1969 to cover the large budget deficits that only recently have ended.

Common Bonds Among Bonds

Bonds are not unlike cars. Even though cars come from different manufacturers and there are many makes and models in hundreds of colors to choose from at different prices, each car has a transmission and wheels, and operates on gas fueled by internal combustion—the basic characteristics that apply across the board. So, too, with bonds.

Every bond issued is either secured or unsecured. A secured bond is backed by specific assets of the borrower, which can be sold to repay the lender if the borrower goes belly-up and defaults. Mortgage-backed bonds and equipment trust certificates would be examples of secured bonds. Unsecured bonds (called debentures) are those backed only by the full faith and credit of the borrower. T-bonds fall into this category, and are the safest of all bonds because the federal government has never defaulted on a loan and is unlikely to; it can, if necessary, print more money to continue payments.

Most corporate bonds are unsecured also, but when issued by reliable institutions such as the Dow 30 Industrials, they are reasonably safe, too. Many corporate borrowers, however, to make their unsecured bonds more attractive to the lending public, often add some frosting, called a conversion privilege. They issue convertible bonds, which give investors the option of exchanging at some point their unsecured corporate bonds for a specific number of shares of common stock in the company, as a guarantee of repayment on the loan instead of receiving cash.

Bonds come either in bearer or registered form. Ownership of a bearer bond is simply ascribed to whoever bears (holds) the bond in his or her possession; thus it is highly negotiable, like cash. Bearer bonds have coupons attached. Each coupon—another word for interest in bond jargon—represents a scheduled interest payment due from the borrower. On most bonds, payments are due twice a year. At the appropriate time, the bearer whips out the scissors, clips the coupon from the bond certificate, and sends it in to receive payment.

Virtually all bonds in this country used to be sold in bearer form, and many bearer bonds are still in wide circulation today. But with the passage of the Tax Reform Act of 1982, bond buyers could finally put the scissors away, as bonds no longer come with detachable coupons and are registered in the holder's name. When semiannual interest payments are due from the borrower, they're automatically sent to the bondholder whose name appears on the borrower's books.

Most 30-year corporate and many municipal bonds include a call provision. This is a string attached that gives the borrower the option, within a certain number of years (usually five or ten), of paying off the bond before its scheduled maturity date. Should interest rates drop significantly, the issuer can then save money by floating new bonds at the lower market rates. It's basically the same strategy as refinancing your home mortgage if market rates fall in order to reduce the size of your monthly interest payments. If the bond is called, the investor is typically paid a premium (a figure slightly higher than the bond's face value) as compensation for the loss of long-term steady income, the result of the debt's being retired early. T-bonds tend not to have call provisions, another big advantage to them in terms of greater investor protection.

How Bonds Work

Bonds are issued in denominations of $1,000 and increments of $5,000 thereafter. This is called their face, or par, value—the full amount of the loan to be paid back when the bond reaches maturity. Maturities on bonds range from ten to thirty years. Bonds with maturities under 10 years are called notes.

The interest rate the bond pays is the percentage of par value returned to the bondholder in fixed, semiannual installments until the bond matures and the debt is retired; it represents the issuer's cost of borrowing the money and the investor's reward for lending it. For example, if a $1,000 bond is paying a coupon rate of 12 percent per annum, this means the investor would receive $120 each year in interest (paid semiannually in installments of $60 apiece) until the bond matures.

The interest rate determines the actual price of the bond to the investor, and is influenced by several factors. The first is the demand to borrow money. When the demand by governments and corporations to issue public debt is high, the cost (interest rate paid) of borrowing that money goes up. When the demand is low, the cost goes down.

The second factor is the risk/reward ratio. The more risk assumed in buying a particular bond, the greater the reward (higher the interest rate) the investor expects to receive.

Anticipated changes in the rate of inflation over the long haul is one way investors have of assessing the risk/reward ratio. For example, if inflation picks up, the prices of goods and services in the economy go up too, taking interest rates with them. This can make the value of existing bonds—the fixed rate of return the investor is locked into—potentially less attractive than that of comparable long-term securities. (For a more detailed discussion of this and other elements of bond risk, see Chapter 6.) Conversely, slow inflation and actual deflation are friends of bonds.

A less speculative method of assessing the risk/reward ratio is to look at a bond's credit rating. This is a letter ranking, or grade, used by independent services such as Standard & Poor's and Moody's to gauge the issuer's potential to repay the loan in the future (see Table 2.1). Ratings are based on the financial stability of the issuer, which these services continually monitor.

Because the federal government's debt obligations are viewed as being free of default risk, T-bonds are not rated by these services. They're judged to be the highest-quality bonds available, and serve as the benchmark against which all other bonds are rated and priced.

The higher the rating, the more stable the issuer, whose bonds are considered "Investment Grade." Likewise, the higher the bond's rating, the lower its interest rate generally will be; there is

Table 2.1
Bond Ratings

Moody's	S&P's	What They Mean
Aaa	AAA	The highest-quality, lowest-risk bonds.
Aa	AA	High-quality debt obligations with minimal repayment risk.
A	A	Quality bonds with a strong capacity to pay interest and principal but are somewhat susceptible to adverse economic conditions.
Baa	BBB	Quality bonds with adequate capacity to pay interest and principal but are more vulnerable to adverse economic conditions.
Ba	BB	Medium-grade bonds with few desirable characteristics.
B	B	Speculative bonds with a major degree of risk in adverse economic conditions.
Caa	CCC	Issuers in poor standing.
Ca	CC	Issuers may be in default.
C	C	Income bonds on which no interest is being paid.
—	D	Bonds in default.

no need for such high-caliber issuers to pay more to borrow money, due to their sound financial footing. Issuers of lower-rated and unrated bonds such as "junk" bonds, on the other hand, will tend to offer higher rates in order to entice investors, particularly those of the "no guts, no glory" stripe.

Interest Versus Yield

The coupon interest rate paid on a bond is not the same as its yield, which refers to the rate of return actually *earned* on the actual amount invested in the bond. Depending upon how much the market price of a bond fluctuates—gains or loses value—over time, its yield can be higher or lower than its coupon interest rate at different points.

There are three types of yield: nominal, current, and yield to maturity.

Nominal yield is the amount of fixed income returned on a bond annually, or its coupon rate expressed as a percent. On a $1,000 bond with a coupon rate of 12 percent, that would be $120 per year, or a nominal yield of 12 percent. Regardless of how much a bond's market price fluctuates, its nominal yield always remains the same.

Fluctuations in the market price of a bond do affect its current yield, however, which is the actual income rate of return, also expressed as a percent, based on the bond's market value if bought or sold today. Current yield is calculated by dividing the annual interest on a bond by its current market price. Using our previous example of a $1,000 bond paying 12 percent trading at par (no change in market price), our current yield is 12 percent. But if the market price of that same bond goes down and it is traded at a discount of, say, $800 ($200 less than par), then our current yield is 15 percent. Conversely, if the bond is currently trading at a premium of $1,200 ($200 above par), then our current yield is only 10 percent. In other words, the more a bond goes for on the secondary market, the less your current yield, and vice versa.

Yield to maturity is the most precise way of measuring the real return of a bond (compared to other types of fixed-income and long-term securities) because it takes everything into account: coupon rate in relation to price, purchase price versus par value, and the amount of time left to maturity when the bond is redeemed. Therefore, it is also the most complicated. It's best to have your broker provide this information; but for those do-it-yourselfers out there, here are the respective formulas for calculating yield to maturity, first on a bond bought at a discount (below face value), and second on a bond bought at a premium (above face value).

Table 2.2
Calculating Yield to Maturity

Discount Bond
Par Value = $1,000
Purchase Price = $800
Coupon Rate (dollar amount of annual interest) = $120
Prorated Discount ($200 ÷ 20) = $10
Theoretical Average Price = ($1,000 + $800) ÷ 2 = $900
Yield to Maturity = ($120 + $10) ÷ $900 = 0.144444
Yield to Maturity = 0.144444 100 × 14.4 percent

Premium Bond
Par Value = $1,000
Purchase Price = $1,200
Coupon Rate = $120
Prorated Premium ($200 ÷ 20) = $10
Theoretical Average Price = ($1,000 + $1,200) ÷ 2 = $1,100
Yield to Maturity = ($120 – $10) ÷ $1,100 = 0.10
Yield to Maturity = 0.1 × 100 = 10 percent

Let's use our $1,000 bond at 12 percent as the example and say it has a thirty-year maturity and we've held it for ten years. To figure the prorated discount or premium figure used in each formula, simply take the discount or premium paid on the bond and divide it by the number of years left until the bond matures, in this case, twenty (see Table 2.2).

Buying and Selling Bonds

Corporate and municipal bonds are traded on a commission basis by most securities brokers and commercial banks.

T-bonds can also be bought and sold through banks and securities dealers for a nominal fee, or without paying a fee through Federal Reserve Banks or the government's Bureau of Public Debt, which has set up a Treasury Direct program for investors who find paying commissions too onerous and other sources of buying and selling too much of a hassle.

With Treasury Direct, individual investors who want to purchase, redeem, or reinvest all kinds of Treasury securities can call 1-800-943-6864 and establish an account. Principal and interest payments are made electronically by direct deposit to the bank of their choice.

Unlike most municipal and corporate bonds, which are traded over the counter, prices of most outstanding (previously issued) U.S. Treasury bonds traded on the secondary market are posted daily in the pages of the financial press and most major newspapers around the country (see Table 2.3).

New T-bonds are sold through Federal Reserve Banks at auctions where prices are determined by competitive bid. These auctions are generally held the second week of February, August, and November, and issued to purchasers on the fifteenth of those months, unless the fifteenth falls on a weekend or holiday, in which case the securities are issued the following business day.

Information about upcoming auctions can be obtained by contacting the thirty-six Federal Reserve Banks that handle Treasury securities, or the government's Bureau of Public Debt Web site on the Internet (http://www.publicdebt.treas.gov).

Federal Reserve Banks

FRB Atlanta	FRB Baltimore	FRB Birmingham
404-521-8653	410-576-3300	205-731-8708
FRB Boston	FRB Buffalo	FRB Charlotte
617-973-3810	716-849-5000	704-358-2424

FRB Chicago	FRB Cincinnati	FRB Cleveland
312-322-5369	513-721-4794	216-579-2000
FRB Dallas	FRB Denver	FRB Detroit
214-922-6100	303-572-2473	313-964-6157
FRB El Paso	FRB Houston	FRB Jacksonville
915-521-8272	713-659-4433	904-632-1179
FRB Kansas City	FRB Little Rock	FRB Los Angeles
816-881-2883	501-324-8272	213-624-7398
FRB Louisville	FRB Memphis	FRB Miami
502-568-9238	901-523-7171	305-471-6497
FRB Minneapolis	FRB Nashville	FRB New Orleans
612-204-6650	615-251-7225	504-593-3200
FRB New York	FRB Oklahoma City	FRB Omaha
212-720-6619	405-270-8652	402-221-5636
FRB Philadelphia	FRB Pittsburgh	FRB Portland
215-574-6680	412-261-7802	503-221-5932
FRB Richmond	FRB St. Louis	FRB Salt Lake City
804-697-8372	314-444-8703	801-322-7882
FRB San Antonio	FRB San Francisco	FRB Seattle
210-978-1305	415-974-2330	206-343-3605

Why Invest in Bonds?

Here are a couple of quotes about the relative merits of stocks and bonds as speculations, recorded at different points in history and

Table 2.3
How to Read the T-bond Tables
Treasury Bonds

Rate	Maturity Mo/Yr	Bid	Asked	Chg	Ask Yld
11¾	Feb 01	116:17	116:21	+3	5.53
14¼	Feb 02	129:28	130:02	+4	5.64
10¾	May 03	122:11	122:17	+9	5:67
12	May 05	135:29	136:03	+10	5.79

Rate: The bond's annual rate of interest expressed as a percent of par value.

Mo/Yr: Maturity, the month and year the bond comes due (e.g., Feb 01 = February 2001).

Bid: The price, expressed as a percent of par value, traders were willing to pay for the bond that day.

Asked: The price, expressed as a percent of par value, traders were willing to sell the bond for that day.

Chg: The difference between the latest asked price of the bond compared to the previous day's price expressed in 32nds of a percent, plus or minus.

Ask Yld: The bond's yield to maturity, expressed as a percent, if traded that day.

*Source: The *Wall Street Journal*.

reflecting different economic times, the first circa the 1929–1932 crash and the second from the big bull market era of today:

- "Common stocks, as such, are not superior to bonds as long-term investments, because primarily they are not investments at all. They are speculations."*

*From *Investments and Speculations* by Lawrence Chamberlain and William H. Hay, 1932.

- "The more data we analyze, the more confident we are that stocks are superior long-term investments. In the long run, the true risk resides with fixed-income investments [bonds], not with common stocks."*

As a contemporary money maven, not one of long ago and far away, how can I reconcile the inherent contradictions of these opposing views and suggest that bonds should be an option that even today's stocks-only crowd should always consider?

The U.S. government has been floating bonds to the public since the 1790s, and American companies have been issuing them for almost as long. So, the reason bonds were held in much higher regard than stocks during the early years of this century was that, in the experience of most investors, who tend to be creatures of habit, common stocks were felt to be too much of a gamble. This was so even though in terms of total return—capital gains plus income—the wealth-producing potential of stocks over the longer term has always been greater than that of bonds.

Bonds started to gain favor when the Roaring Twenties' big bull market in stocks ended on October 24, 1929, day one of that nightmarish period in American history called the Great Crash, when so many dice-rolling investors lost their all-too-tight-fitting financial shirts.

For example, if these same investors had followed banker and U.S. Treasury Secretary (1921–1932) Andrew Mellon's early warning (immortalized in his famous wordplay on the title of Anita Loos's flapper-era comedy, *Gentlemen Prefer Blondes*, that heads this chapter), and before the Great Crash had put their money in long-term government bonds rather than stocks, their financial fate at the end of it would have been very different. They would have gotten back their original investment, plus an additional 13.8 percent in cumulative interest. In other words, not only would they have dodged a helluva bullet (Howitzer shell, really), they would have

---

*From *Stocks for the Long Run* by Jeremy Siegel, 1994.

turned bust into boom and *made money*. By the same token, if they'd bought stocks, they would have lost almost 90 percent of their money in nominal terms, and almost 75 percent in current (real) terms, and probably jumped from a high window, as so many did.

It is only after an out-of-favor investment has performed well for a long period of time that it again becomes popular. The legacy of the Great Crash, which made the investing public even more leery of stocks and even more enamored of bonds than ever before, lasted almost forty years.

The low regard of bonds as an appealing investment, despite their steady returns and inherent safety, and rabid endorsement of stocks as the long-term investment of choice in America are fairly recent phenomena. Basically, the turnaround was born of President Lyndon Johnson's "Guns and Butter" Vietnam and Great Society policies, wherein Mr. Johnson decided to fight a war against the communist insurgency in Southeast Asia and a war on poverty at the same time *without raising taxes*.

At that time—1968—America was running at under 4 percent unemployment and using 90 percent of its factory capacity. So, when Mr. Johnson stepped on the economic accelerator, only one thing could happen. Because suddenly there was more demand chasing a lesser supply of goods and services, prices went up. As a result, inflation, which had historically not been much of a problem in our country, except for short periods—generally during wartime—became endemic.

As I've written, inflation is the enemy of bonds over the long haul, whereas the value of stocks tends to outpace inflation in the long term. In the aftermath of Mr. Johnson's economic and military adventure—or misadventure, as the case may be—through the 1970s and early 1980s when inflation reached double digits, investors began to assume that inflation at such levels was *normal*, and bonds came to be viewed almost as "certificates of confiscation."

Meanwhile stocks began their ascendancy. Whereas stocks had previously sold quite cheaply in relation to bonds, the situation reversed in 1968, and bonds became cheaper than stocks for the first time in this century. In fact, this condition has persisted for twenty-one out of the last twenty-nine years.

However, inflation at such levels was and is abnormal in our economy. And today inflation has practically been eliminated as a matter of much concern at all in our country. In fact, our economy may be entering a period of possible deflation. Even so normally cautious a reader of economic tea leaves as Federal Reserve Chairman Alan Greenspan has gone on record and voiced this possibility due to the number of portents he sees out there. Products and services in many areas of our economy *are* getting cheaper.

The price of computers, that prime fixture of the booming consumer electronics industry, is just one example. Today you can buy an extremely powerful computer with all the bells and whistles for under $1,000, whereas just a couple years ago, a computer with a fraction of those capabilities would have cost you $2,000. Oil and cars are falling in price as well. When the price of its products drops, a company's profits do, too, which is bad for its stock, shrinking or eliminating the dividend income that stockholders look for and expect from their investment. If slumping prices begin to pervade an economy, and hold on, even for a while, the comparatively lower but fixed and steady income returned by bonds will seem not such a bad alternative.

There are those who believe that deflation on such a scale simply couldn't happen here. Maybe not. But against all seeming odds, it happened to that once mighty economic behemoth Japan, which is now in its ninth year of a deflationary period caused by stiff overseas competition, an overvalued stock market, and other factors. So, who's to say?

Stocks in this country have yielded a higher rate of return since the 1980s than during the entire 180 years such financial data has been recorded. This has led a greater number of people to believe the stock market *always* goes up, and to invest an increasing amount of their money in stocks, resulting in a kind of self-fulfilling prophecy whereby the more money that goes in, the more stocks go up, attracting a greater number of people to put a greater percentage of their net worth into the stock market each year.

If you follow this through to its logical conclusion, how are today's "Stocks 'R' Us" investors going to react when the market makes another of its historically cyclical corrections? Many of them belong to a generation so unfamiliar with a downturn (that lasts more than couple of days, anyway) that they feel a prolonged stock market reversal of fortune could happen only in an episode of *The Twilight Zone*.

In the same manner that these investors have overreacted to the big bull market of the past several decades—an extended run that is not only unusual but completely unprecedented in our country's history—and pushed stocks up too high, they'll probably do what their forerunners did after the 1929–1932 Great Crash. Shift to bonds; and for a considerable amount of time thereafter, it will be difficult to give stocks away. The whole cycle will begin again until a point is reached when bonds are grossly overvalued in relation to price and stocks are grossly undervalued. In that sense, the opposing views presented earlier are both right. It all falls down to which page of the economic calendar is turning, and the investor's astuteness in reading it sufficiently ahead of time to heed the fine print. (Chapter 10 will show you how.)

During long periods of prosperity such as the one we've been experiencing, there's very little interest in being a lender. Companies have done so well for so long and rewarded their shareholders so generously, the lower returns usually available with bonds may seem infinitely less rewarding. But bonds, especially T-bonds, have the advantage in terms of paying more in stable income over time. This income stream is exempt from state and local (but not federal) taxes, a big plus to investors who live in high-tax states or localities. And you know your full investment is going to be there at the end when you need it, whether it's to be used for retirement, sending your kids to college, or whatever purpose.

These advantages, coupled with what history has shown us, confirm my contrarian argument that stocks do not have an inherent superiority over bonds, because there are definitely times when bonds are *the most attractive* place to be.

THREE

Treasury Bills Can Be More Fun

With STOCKS AND BONDS throwing off double-digit returns consistently since 1981, the current 5.25 percent returns of U.S. Treasury bills seem hardly worth consideration. But as Winston Churchill once said, "If you want to look forward further, you look back further." So, as I keep emphasizing, let's not ignore history. But I'm getting a bit ahead of myself. First, a primer on T-bills.

What Are T-bills?

The most widely used of all U.S. Government securities, and a primary instrument of Federal Reserve policy, T-bills, like T-bonds, are issued to the public at a guaranteed rate of interest to pay off maturing debt and to raise more cash for operating the federal government, which backs them with its full faith and credit.

There is no investment in the world where the return of principal is more assured. Because of this, T-bills generally produce lower returns than corporate issues of comparable maturities, or competing, albeit chancier, investment options like stocks—with which there is *no* assurance that one's principal will be returned, and arguably little current return on that principal while waiting. But given the fact that equities can often produce substantial gains, investors in T-bills pay for this safety net, since the flip side of not being able to lose a lot of money is the inability to make as much, either.

How T-bills Work

Similar to zero coupon bonds, T-bills return no interest to the investor until maturity. But unlike bonds in general, T-bills mature very quickly.

The most commonly issued is the 3-month (90-day) bill. But 6-month (180-day) and 12-month (1-year) T-bills are issued as well. All are sold at a discount from par value in minimum denominations of $1,000 to a ceiling of $1 million. The difference between the T-bill's discounted purchase price and its par value is your return.

For example, if you buy a 1-year T-bill sold at a discount of 5 percent, your purchase price would be 95 percent of the bill's $1,000 par value, or $950. When the bill matures, you get back your $950 plus $50 interest earned on your investment in the course of that year.

However, there have been occasions—the Depression, for example—when T-bills were sold not at a discount but a premium, a price above par value, returning, in effect, a negative rate of interest.

An indicator of how risk-averse investors can be (and until the big bull era of today have tended to be), this rare but not unrepeatable phenomenon occurred when many of the nation's banks were going under, and Americans were greatly concerned about the viability of such institutions as a secure depository for their hard-earned cash. Not cottoning to the idea of stashing it under a mattress or secreting it in a hole in the ground, people looked upon guaranteed T-bills as their soundest option, and were willing to buy at a premium, seeing their negative return as sort of a storage fee paid to the government to keep their money out of harm's way.

Calculating Yields

Two mathematical formulas can be employed to calculate yields on 90-day, 180-day, and 1-year T-bills. Both use the investor's return (difference between purchase price and par value) in the calculation. But the first, called the Discount Yield method, takes into account the bill's return as a percent of its par value, not its purchase price, to determine annual yield. The second, known as the Investment Yield method, relates return to purchase price to determine current yield, so that investors can compare the security's attractiveness to other short-term investments available on the open market and assess "opportunity risk"—what the same amount of money might earn elsewhere.

Both methods are fairly straightforward and can be easily figured on your own. To see how they work, let's use an example of a T-bill sold at a discounted price of $9,800 and maturing at $10,000 in either 90 days, 180 days, or 1 year. In the Discount Yield method, the approximate number of days in the year used for calculating is 360; it's 365 (366 if a leap year) in the Investment Yield method (see Table 3.1).

Buying and Selling T-bills

T-bills can be traded without paying a fee through Federal Reserve banks and the government's Treasury Direct program (see Chapter 2), as well as through brokerages and the secondary market for a commission.

Table 3.1

Discount Yield Method

90-Day T-bill

$10,000 − $9,800 ÷ $10,000 × 360 ÷ 90 = 0.08 × 100, or
  8 percent annual yield

180-day T-bill

$10,000 − $9,800 ÷ $10,000 × 360 ÷ 180 = 0.04 × 100, or
  4 percent annual yield

1-year T-bill

$10,000-$9,800 ÷ $10,000 × 360 ÷ 360 = 0.02 × 100, or
  2 percent annual yield

Investment Yield Method

90-Day T-bill

$10,000 − $9,800 ÷ $9,800 × 365 ÷ 90 = 0.0827664 × 100, or
  8.28 percent current yield

180-day T-bill

$10,000 − $9,800 ÷ $9,800 × 365 ÷ 180 = 0.0413832 × 100, or
        4.14 percent current yield

1-year T-bill

$10,000-$9,800 ÷ $9,800 × 365 ÷ 365 = 0.0204081 × 100, or
  2.04 percent current yield

New 3-month and 6-month bills are auctioned weekly, on a Monday, and issued the following Thursday, except for holidays and special circumstances. Twelve-month bills are auctioned monthly on a Thursday, and issued a week later, under the same conditions.

Along with interest rates, competitive bids from the larger financial institutions who buy T-bills on a regular basis determine the discount at which new issues are traded at auction. Individual investors can submit competitive bids as well, specifying discount terms, but risk being denied a purchase if their bid doesn't fall within the range accepted at auction. Most individual investors find it easier to submit noncompetitive bids, whereby they agree to go along with the prevailing auction rate in exchange for being guaranteed an issue.

Previously issued obligations are listed daily in the *Wall Street Journal* as well as most newspapers, and weekly in *Barron's* (see Table 3.2).

Table 3.2
How to Read the T-bill Tables

Treasury Bills

Maturity	Days to Mat	Bid	Asked	Chg	Ask Yld
Nov 12 '98	248	5.10	5.08	−0.03	5.30
Dec 10 '98	276	5.10	5.08	−0.03	5.31
Jan 07 '99	304	5.11	5.09	−0.02	5.34
Feb 04 '99	332	5.12	5.10	−0.03	5.36
Mar 04 '99	360	5.11	5.10	−0.02	5.38

Maturity: The date when the debt obligation plus interest are due. It is given to identify the specific T-bill because of the sheer volume of bills issued so closely together.
Days to Mat: The number of days left until redemption. These are all 1-year bills.
Bid: The discounted price from par, expressed as an annualized percentage discount rate, that securities dealers were willing to pay for T-bills that day.
Asked: The discounted price from par, expressed as an annualized percentage discount rate, that securities dealers were willing to sell T-bills for that day.

Table 3.2 (cont.)

Chg: The average rise or fall in the rate of discount from par bid on T-bills during that day's trading session, expressed as a percent, plus or minus. A plus sign signifies an increase in the discount; and a minus sign, a drop. The higher the discount, the lower the price.

Ask Yld: The bill's yield to maturity, expressed as a percent, based on its discount from par if traded that day.

*Source: The *Wall Street Journal*.

Why Invest in T-bills?

As is the case with all U.S. Government securities, T-bills are exempt from state and local, but not federal, income taxes. An added incentive for buying 1-year T-bills is that you can defer the interest on your federal income taxes into the next year—even beyond!

Let's say you buy the bill in January 1999. It wouldn't reach maturity until January 2000, so you wouldn't have to pay income on the interest you receive until April 15, 2001. In essence, that gives you a two-and-a-half-year free ride on the government's money!

T-bills are also highly liquid investment vehicles. If, for some reason, you needed to get your hands on your money before the bill matures, any loss you might suffer for trading early would be minimal, especially on shorter-term bills like the 90-day, because fluctuations in their discounted price due to inflation during such a short amount of time would likely be quite small.

That's the real beauty of T-bills in a nutshell: their virtual immunity to volatility when held to such short-term maturity. It's also the numero uno concern if you're a safety-first investor who finds the volatility inherent in long-term vehicles such as stocks too nerve-fraying.

Inclined to make an incorrect move out of panic whenever markets go down, and potentially lose money they can ill afford, safety-first investors *know* they don't have the financial cushion to take the long-term view.

This may unfortunately prove to be the case as well with many of today's so-called long-term investors, who have yet to be tested under adverse conditions to find out just how long-term they really are. They may, I suspect, flee the riskier financial markets when the going gets tough and they discover their financial cushion doesn't have much padding, either.

For example, if you're receiving a 7 percent stock dividend per year, you can afford to lose 7 percent of your capital if the market heads south, and still break even. But if the price/earnings ratio has pushed dividends down to 1.6 percent, as is the case in today's overvalued stock market, that doesn't leave much margin for error, particularly when 1, 2, and 3 percent stock market declines are quite common nowadays. Then panic time sets in.

Particularly during periods of severe inflation, when not only bonds but stocks tend do poorly, low-risk/low-return T-bills, while by no means unaffected by inflation, can be the investor's salvation due to their short-term maturities.

Such times have been numerous in our century. For example, in the high inflation years of 1968 to 1981, T-bills outperformed both stocks and bonds by a wide margin, as seen in Figure 3.1.

If you had bought T-bills and rolled them over throughout this thirteen-year period, you would have had a total cumulative return of more than 150 percent compared to just under 59 percent for bonds and under 104 percent for stocks. In other words, you would have beaten stocks by 47 percentage points and bonds by 90 percentage points—with complete safety, security, and continuity.

Record Returns

Whereas T-bills have historically paid, on the average, a half a percent in real interest—that's interest above inflation—today, a 90-

day bill pays around 5.25 percent, at a time when trailing twelve month's inflation is 1.4 percent, or hardly a blip on the economic radar screen. That means T-bill investors are getting a bit more than 3.5 percent real interest, or almost *double* the historical return, on a security that is basically riskless due to its total safety from default. (Nevertheless, while free of default risk, T-bills are not immune to all risk, a subject I'll get to in Chapter 7.)

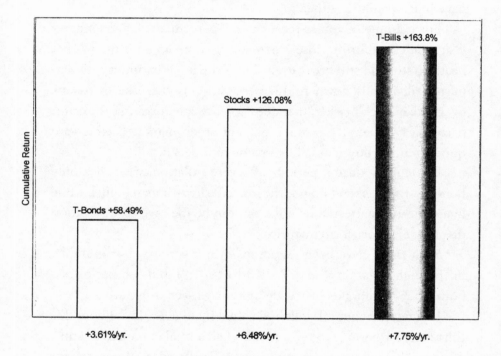

Figure 3.1. High Inflation, 1968–1981.

Yet the majority of today's investors are putting the bulk of their money into stocks paying current dividends of only 1.6 percent, with a very high potential for loss. This is a clear sign of the low regard in which super safe T-bills are held now; despite today's historic 5.25 percent returns, investors are looking at the risk/reward ratio of T-bills and saying, "That's not enough reward even for so little risk!"

But 5.25 percent is a *very* high rate of return; today's T-bill investors are now harvesting in just *three months* what, historically, their ancestors would have had to go out *thirty years* or more to harvest from these securities.

The obvious conclusion is that during poor economic times, when investors have to be more concerned with the safe return rather than enhancement of their principal, that Rodney Dangerfield of the investment world that gets so little respect, the lowly T-bill, unless bought at a premium, can be awfully effective, and may, in fact, be the *value* place to be.

With my new strategy to be revealed later in this book, you'll discover a very simple way of determining those times—when to get in, when to get out. But here's a preview: In the last twenty-nine years, T-bills have outperformed at least one of their competitors, stocks or bonds; and in nine of the last twenty-nine years—roughly one-third of the time—outperformed both. My new strategy would have had you buying 1-year T-bills and holding them until maturity, in ten of the past twenty-nine years!

Now let's make the case for stocks.

FOUR

Stocks Have Their Place, Too

DESPITE THEIR CURRENT LEVEL OF GROSS OVERVALUATION, common stocks must *always* be considered as a possible investment option because, when reinvested dividends are included, stocks normally bury all other liquid investment alternatives over long periods of time.

A look at Figure 4.1 tells the whole story in considerably less than a thousand words.

Even accounting for inflation, if you'd bought a portfolio of large or small company common stocks at the end of 1925, the first year accurate records became available, every dollar you put in would have grown in reinvested value to $1,828.33 or $5,519.97, respectively, by year-end 1997—versus $39.07 for every dollar put in the long-term government bond market, and a mere $14.35 in T-bills.

So, dollar for dollar, the compounded effect of investing in stocks over more modestly returning T-bonds and T-bills during the past seventy-plus years has been enormous, soaring them to the top of the heap in our pyramid of chosen investment options.

But there are shifting sands beneath that pyramid that can cause

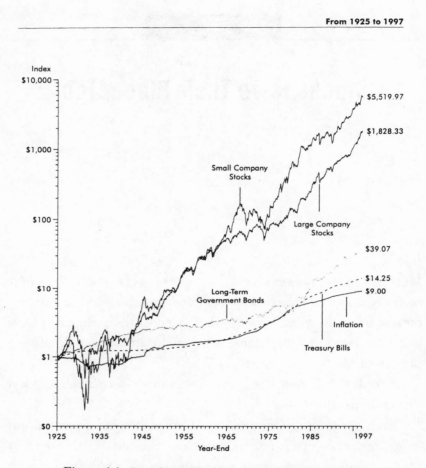

Figure 4.1. Cumulative Wealth Indices of Common Stocks, Government, Corporate, and Municipal Bonds, and T-Bills, 1925–1997.

the distance between top and bottom to narrow. Furthermore, if you look at a drawing of a pyramid on paper, what's the top from one angle isn't the top from another, depending upon where you're standing.

Clearly, if you want to make money—*big* money—you're definitely better off speculating in stocks than investing in T-bonds and T-bills, provided you can stay in the game for the long haul. But the operative words are "long haul," for every game has a season.

In the short term (particularly five years or less), stocks, as I've shown in earlier chapters, can go down big-time, producing losses instead of gains, and falling behind T-bonds and T-bills.

The Privileges of Ownership

A company issues common stock for a host of reasons. As with bonds, the objective is to raise money—although the goal with stocks is to accomplish this by not adding more debt to the books. In fact, the company may even want the money for liquidating existing debt.

Some common reasons companies have for issuing stocks to rustle up cash include: developing a new line of products; expanding inventory; building new plants here and abroad; modernizing existing ones; financing a merger with a like-minded company for a strong one-two punch in the marketplace; bankrolling the acquisition of a pesky competitor to achieve market dominance; and attracting, rewarding, or retaining key employees.

In return for buying a company's common stock, the purchaser gains fundamental ownership equity in that enterprise, and is enti-

tled to most if not all of the privileges that go with ownership. For example, stockholders can participate in the election of the company's board of directors, as well as vote, in person or by proxy, on corporate plans and policies affecting business, and thus their own fortunes as stockholders.

So, one important thing stock ownership can do for you is get you the ear of someone like General Electric CEO Jack Welch—though how much he'll listen will depend on how big a GE shareholder you are. To paraphrase George Orwell: All stockholders are equal, but some are more equal than others. The bigger your investment, the more say you have. Or, put another way, it's not the squeakiest wheel that gets the most grease in stock ownership, but the one with the most tread—unless it's the same wheel.

But the most important reward of stock ownership is sharing in the company's profits if they smash through the roof—though again, how much of this wealth you'll be entitled to depends on the number of shares in your portfolio as a percentage of shares outstanding. The greater your percentage, the heftier your profit participation, which can be paid out as quarterly dividends or reinvested in the business or, usually, some combination of both.

Just as with corporate and government bond income, which is paid out as interest, dividend earnings on stocks are taxable, not just federally but across the board. This is one of the reasons some companies, usually smaller, growing ones, elect not to pay dividends, but automatically reinvest stockholder earnings in the company's operations instead. This alternative form of payment can increase the long-term capital gain of the stockholder's investment in the company, and the size of participation in future windfalls as well, big pluses both.

Another reason a company may elect to reinvest rather than pay stockholder dividends is to avoid floating more issues of stock in the first place, as this can be costly and also dilutes the profits spread among stockholders, whose ranks would be increased. Some larger corporations offer Dividend Reinvestment Plans (called DRIPs) for many of the same reasons.

Hand in hand with the privilege of being rewarded handsomely if a company's wealth blossoms comes risk if it wilts; stockholders bear the heaviest brunt of this risk, potentially sacrificing much, if not all, of their investment if the company's profit picture gets a mite grainy, falls out of focus, or just plain fails to develop. In fact, if the company goes bust and has to liquidate assets, holders of common stock are paid last in line after preferred shareholders and creditors such as bondholders.

If profits head south, the investor's dividend checks may follow the same route; the company may even suspend paying dividends for a while until things improve. Normally, the value of the stockholder's investment, as reflected in the stock's falling market price, heads south, too.

Under such conditions, the more shares you own, the more of a hit you take, especially if you panic when prices are down and sell at a loss. (Conversely, buying a company's stock when prices are down can ultimately produce big gains—depending on the company, of course—and is the strategy I always recommend.) But holding out can make for a long and bumpy ride; losses may not be permanent but substantial, depending upon the length of time it takes for the company to regain its sea legs, return to the black, and see the market value of its stock shoot up again. Conceivably it could be years before the company's stock reaches the same valuation level it had before it fell and the investor is back to par. This is an element of stock investment risk that applies not only to individual stocks, but even more intricately, to the market as a whole. This will be explained further in the next chapter, as well as put in a historical context so that you can better understand where the market has been, and where it may be headed.

Just keep in mind that volatility is a fundamental characteristic of the stock market, and some stocks are more volatile than others, which is why stock ownership is not for the fair-weather player or the timorous. A basic rule of thumb: No matter how good the stock-picking system (even mine) may be, you shouldn't invest any more in common stocks than you can reasonably afford to relinquish in the short term without significantly altering your lifestyle.

Buying and Selling Stocks

Common stocks are bought and sold through full-service or discount brokerage firms that trade daily on the major exchanges. The broker charges a commission to your account for each transaction; rates differ according to the value of the stock, volume of shares purchased (or sold), and the type of broker it is. Generally, the amount of commission declines as volume increases.

Full-service brokers charge a fairly high commission rate due to the extensive amount of customer advice and hand-holding they provide. Befitting their name, discount brokers offer only the buy-and-sell basics, so they charge a lower commission rate, though how much lower will vary from discounter to discounter. Most charge a minimum commission (usually around $25) for transactions under $1,000, but recently, Internet brokers have begun charging as little as $8 per transaction.

Whether full-service or discounter, all legitimate brokers carry insurance on customer accounts up to $500,000, a legal requirement aimed at protecting customers from losses due to a brokerage's failure to fulfill its obligations, or to the failure of the brokerage itself. This insurance is bought through Securities Protection Investor Corporation (SPIC), an organization funded by member brokers. Most firms carry other insurance as well.

Which type of broker is best for you depends on your degree of risk tolerance and level of confidence in understanding and navigating the investment world. But one of the goals of my first book, as well as this one, is to provide you with all the information you need in one place; to enable you to do as much as possible of the real spade work comfortably on your own, so you can then just place your order, whether it's for stocks, T-bonds, or T-bills.

Stock Valuation

The best time to buy a stock is after it's gone down a great deal in price and is cheap, so that you get more value for your money, similar to hitting a hot sale at Macy's. It is also important to comparison shop for the best buy, just as you do at your local grocery store.

Four yardsticks are used to determine whether the price of an individual stock is selling cheaply or too expensively relative to other stocks, and whether the stock market as a whole is over- or underpriced in comparison with the T-bond and T-bill markets.

Price to Earnings Ratio (P/E)

This is one of the best benchmarks for stock valuation because it measures the earning power of a given stock against its current market price. It enables you to relate the current value of the stock to past performance and make a reasonable assessment about how good a performer it will be in the future.

The P/E ratio is calculated by dividing the market price of the stock by the current per share earnings of the company. For example, let's say the common stock of XYZ company is currently selling for $45 per share and has reported earnings of $3 per share over the last year. The stock's P/E ratio ($45 ÷ $3) equals 15.

If, in the past decade, that stock's P/E ratios have been in the single digits on the low side, and around 30 on the high side, its current P/E ratio is historically low; thus the stock may be a good buy because in addition to the possibility of earnings growth, the P/E ratio may expand.

By the same token, if that stock is currently selling at $75 a share and the reported earnings per share are $3, its P/E ratio ($75 ÷ $3) would be 25. That would be on the high side historically, so it may not be as good a buy. If you buy stocks on the high side, it's extremely hard to make money. So, the key is to have an idea of when stocks are expensive or cheap, which calculating and tracking P/E ratios can tell you.

Generally speaking, stocks are cheap at 6 times earnings and expensive at 23 times earnings; historically, those have been the traditional lows and highs. In between, it's important to know whether the market is on the way from 23 to 6, or vice versa. In my view, the market's having gone from a P/E of 6 to a current high P/E (as of this writing) of around 28—which is completely off the charts—indicates that we're probably headed back toward 6 again. Since this pattern in the past has normally occurred in thirteen-year cycles, the next bottom in market P/E ratios will likely occur sometime around the turn of the century.

Price to Book Value Ratio

Book value is what a company's bean counters figure its net assets to be after all debts, claims, and other liabilities are subtracted. In other words, it is an estimate of the fundamental value of the company from an accountant's point of view.

Book value per share is arrived at by adding up everything the company owns, subtracting everything it owes to creditors and preferred shareholders, then dividing by the total number of shares of common stock it has outstanding. Using our fictional company as an example again, let's say XYZ's bean counters have assessed the company's net assets at the end of the last quarter to be $35 million, and its total liabilities to be $11 million, with 600,000 shares outstanding. Here's how the formula works: $35M − $11M = $24M ÷ 600,000 = $40, the book value per share.

But if the market value of XYZ's stock is $36, it's being sold *below* book value, indicating a potentially good buy; investors could walk away with money in their pockets after all the company's obligations are paid off.

However, company bean counters seldom carry the assets of the company at proper value. They tend to base their assessment on the original cost of the company's assets less accumulated depreciation. As a result, book value is somewhat theoretical as an indicator of a stock's true value.

However, as a measure of traditional market highs and lows that allows you to gauge how over- or underpriced the market is at a given time, price to book value can be a useful benchmark. In the past, the market was selling cheap at book value or below, and expensive at twice book value. Today, the market is selling at over 6 times book value—again, way off the charts. But if it ever gets down to below book value again, that would certainly be an indication of a cheap stock market, one that is likely to produce above-normal returns. And it's not so long ago—in the late 1970s and early 1980s, just at the beginning of this big bull market—that stocks *were* selling below book value, on the Dow anyway. So, it's not as if we're talking ancient history so far removed from our experience that a repetition seems wholly inconceivable.

Dividend Yield Ratio

This is the yardstick I personally consider to be the most reliable as an indicator of the reasonableness of a stock's price, certainly for company stocks with long and established dividend yield track records that can put current returns into an historical context. In addition, dividends are not subject to manipulation by accountants the way book value and earnings are. No one can get away with telling you that a $1 dividend is other than what it is. Another advantage to using dividends as a benchmark is that, unlike earnings, they are very stable.

All you have to do to determine dividend yield is take the current annual dividend and divide it by the stock's current market price. Historically, the dividend yield on stocks has ranged between 7 and 7.5 percent on the high side and around 3 percent on the low side. When the big bull market started in 1982, dividend yields in the market were around 7 percent. They're now running at 1.4 percent—extreme overvaluation.

Using XYZ company once more, if it's paying an annual dividend rate of return of $1.60 a share and selling at $45 a share, the dividend yield is about 3.6 percent ($1.60 ÷ $45 = 0.036). This indicates that XYZ's stock is historically on the low side in terms of real return, and therefore overvalued as an investment. On the other hand, as it's running two full percentage points above today's market average, it's less overpriced than most other stocks and a better value, but only relatively so.

Dividend yield, however, is of somewhat limited benefit as a benchmark tool for valuating the common stocks of start-up and young, rapidly growing small companies. Either they're too new to pay dividends, or they choose not to pay them, plowing all of the profits back into the business, instead.

Price to Sales Ratio

This last basis for assessing the value of a stock requires a little homework on the average investor's part, as companys' year-end sales figures are not readily reported in the daily financial press. But they can be easily obtained by getting hold of a company's annual report or subscribing to market references like *Value Line* and Standard & Poor's Stock Guide, which regularly track the sales figures of most companies.

By dividing the amount of sales by the number of shares the company has outstanding, you get a sales per share figure. To get the price to sales ratio, divide the sales per share figure by the stock's current market price. If the price to sales ratio is below 1, that indicates pretty good value, historically.

Types of Stocks

Take a stroll through your home or office and note the number of different products you see and use every day—from computers and other appliances to telephones, furniture, clothing, grooming and medical supplies, groceries, newspapers, and so on, ad infinitum. Each was made by a company that has probably issued stock—perhaps for the purpose of financing the manufacture and marketing of one of the very products you're looking at.

This little exercise gives you some idea of the enormous volume and variety of stocks available from which you can choose. Nevertheless, for all the diversity, every stock basically falls into one of three broad categories, depending upon the size of the issuer and degree of capitalization.

Big Caps

These are the stocks of big companies—so named because the companies are those with total market capitalizations in excess of $1 billion. Some, like AT&T, Coca-Cola, General Electric, General Motors, and McDonald's, to mention but a few, are capitalized to the tune of hundreds of billions. They are the heaviest hitters, the biggest of the big caps, also known as blue chips, the color chips poker players like to win because they're the most valuable stakes in the game.

All blue chips are big caps, but not all big caps are blue chips. The blue chips are the safest of all stocks because of their greater liquidity and because of their enormous size, economic importance, and tremendous staying power, their ability to stand erect in the wind no matter how hard it's blowing from whatever direction. In fact, how well they're standing is usually seen by Wall Street as a sign of how well the market overall is standing—the old adage, "What's good for General Motors is good for the U.S.A." Which is why, when one of the blue chips gets the sniffles, anxiety spreads across Wall Street that the market may be coming down with the flu. So, the blue chips have an enormous impact on the psychology of the market as well.

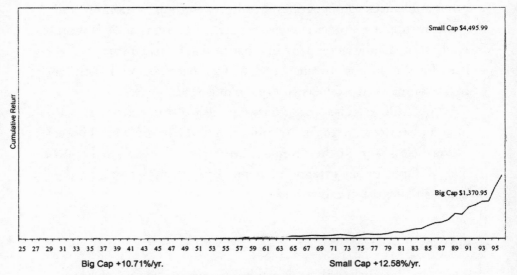

Figure 4.2. Small Cap vs. Big Cap Performance.

Small Caps

However, there are many thousands of smaller or medium-sized but lesser-known companies with capitalizations ranging from under to over $500 million that are available for investment also. These are the small caps. If one has the ability to buy a large number of these stocks and stay with them, the results can be superior to those of the blue chips over time (see Figure 4.2).

Ever since year-end 1925, small cap stocks have beaten blue chip stocks on the average by around two percentage points per year. Over this entire seventy-three-year period, this trend has resulted in a total cumulative return of 449,500 percent for small cap stocks compared to 137,095 percent cumulatively for the S&P 500. Thus, on an aggregate basis, small cap stocks have out-returned big cap stocks by 3.3 times. The reason is that small cap stocks have more room for growth, adaptability, and mobility than big cap stocks.

But small cap performance hasn't always been in a straight line. Small cap stocks have suffered through long periods of dramatic

subpar performance followed by long periods of impressive outper-
formance.

For example, from 1925 through the middle of 1932, an
investor would have lost a devastating 82.5 percent in small caps
while suffering a more modest decline of 51.3 percent in the blue
chips of the Dow and S&P. Likewise, the period 1968 through
1974 witnessed small cap cumulative losses of 58.4 percent compared to only a 28.7 percent shrinkage in larger stocks.

Thus, small cap investing isn't for the faint of heart, or for
many average investors who typically don't have the time to do the
research required to invest in a broad enough cross-section of these
stocks to be sufficiently well diversified. Also, these stocks have a
tendency to be here today, gone tomorrow. They grow faster than
big caps, but because of this they're more volatile, more vulnerable
to competitive pressures that could sink them—conditions big caps
are more prone to survive.

There are definitely cycles when big caps outperform small
caps, and vice versa. That's been the case in eleven of the past fourteen years, which is why I think we're setting up for another
cycle—perhaps even a lengthy one—when small caps will outperform big cap stocks again. These swings historically have occurred
after very long cycles of small cap underperformance, such as the
one we're experiencing now. So, just as it's important to know
when to be in T-bonds, T-bills, or stocks, it's equally important to
know—if stocks are the place to be for the best returns—when to
be in big caps or small caps. I'll address that in the final chapter of
this book.

Foreign Stocks

Overseas stocks are a very important market sector, with more new,
fast-growing companies popping up all the time. This is especially
true of the developing countries of the so-called Third World,

where major opportunities for investment exist because of their exploding economies.

These countries have enormous potential for growth because they encompass 85 percent of the world's population, where the average standard of living is so low that it's almost impossible for them to mature too rapidly. For example, if someone in Indonesia is making $100 a month, a $10-a-month increase is 10 percent. If someone elsewhere is making $2,000 a month—as many workers are in the mature economies of the U.S., Europe, and Japan—a $10-a-month increase would be only one half of one percent. That shows the relationship. Furthermore, as these countries have a rate of population growth probably double that of the developed world, their populations tend to be younger, more energetic, and hungrier. So, it's very clear to me that work in the next century is going to shift more toward the $100-a-month countries than the $2,000-a-month ones.

The big advantage of foreign stocks is that, like small caps versus big caps, they tend to grow faster. The downside is that, depending upon the stability of the country economically and politically, foreign stocks tend to be even riskier and more volatile than small caps here at home.

Furthermore, many foreign stocks do not pay dividends of any consequence. Also, they are dominated by foreign currencies, which means that not only do you have to make a judgment as to whether the individual company's fortunes are rosy-looking, but whether the underlying currency of the country is strong or weak against the dollar. Conceivably, you could buy a foreign stock that is doing very well in that country's currency, but actually lose money when your return is translated into dollars. So, for the average investor, these stocks are even harder to analyze than small caps. Nevertheless, because of their undeniable investment potential, foreign stocks should always be given serious consideration.

The most practical way for an American to invest in foreign stocks is either through a foreign mutual fund offered by a brokerage that specializes in this area, or to buy what are known as

American Depository Receipts (ADRs). These are receipts for shares of stock in overseas companies held by American banks; purchasers are entitled to all dividends and capital gains, just as if they were holding the actual shares. Like U.S. equities, returns on foreign stocks are taxed by Uncle Sam.

Getting Information on Stocks

Most of the calculations you need to assess and track the value of a company's common stock are provided in the summary tables of trading activity on the three major stock exchanges that appear daily in the *Wall Street Journal*, the *New York Times*, *Barron's*, and practically every hometown newspaper in the country (see Table 4.1). Still, it's important for you to know how these calculations are arrived at, and what they mean, so that as you read these tables you can make a knowledgeable judgment about how attractive or unattractive a stock may be in terms of valuation compared with other stocks piquing your interest.

The oldest and largest of these exchanges is the New York Stock Exchange (NYSE), which lists the issues of more than two thousand companies. These companies are usually the biggest, boasting the highest levels of capitalization, which is why the NYSE is referred to universally as the "Big Board."

The second-oldest is the American Stock Exchange (AMEX), which lists the issues of around eight hundred companies, most of them small to medium-sized ones that, because they're smaller, tend to be less profitable and are considered more speculative than those listed on the Big Board. There are some exceptions, of course. For example, most of America's oil and gas companies are traded on the AMEX.

The newest kid on the block is the NASDAQ (National Association of Securities Dealers Automated Quotations) National Market and Small Cap Market exchange, which lists four thousand mostly small cap and foreign company over-the-counter stocks that are also considered somewhat speculative. The NASDAQ serves as a launchpad where many start-up and young companies introduce their stocks to equity hounds sniffing around for the next Intel.

Emerging after World War II and blossoming in the 1970s, the NASDAQ is fast outpacing the AMEX in drawing power, adding most of the emerging and fastest-growing small companies in the exploding technology, medical, and communications fields to its rapidly expanding list—which is rounded out by some large caps traded on the NYSE as well.

The NYSE, AMEX, and NASDAQ table formats are practically the same.

Table 4.1
How to Read the Exchange Tables

52-Week							Vol			Net	
Hi	Lo	Stock	Sym	Div	Yld%	P/E	100s	Hi	Lo	Close	Chg
93½	57½	ABC Corp.	ABC	.90	1.0	22	7966	93½	91	93	+2

From left to right, this table shows that the price for ABC Corporation's stock (or ABC, the Associated Press's abbreviation for the company listed under the "Sym" column) has ranged from a high of 93½ ($93.50 a share) to a low of 57½ ($57.50 a share) over the last twelve months. The stock is currently paying an annual dividend of $.90 per share and yielding 1 percent in real terms. It has a price/earnings ratio of 22. Brokers usually buy stocks in round lots of 100 shares, but can purchase them in odd-lots, too. The figure 7966 was the trading volume that day in hundreds of shares. The highest price for the day was 93½ ($93.50 a share); the low was 91 ($91.00 a share), and the stock closed the session at 93 ($93.00 a share), representing a net change during the course of that day's trading action of 2 points, on the plus side.

The Market Indexes

The most widely used sources of information on stocks are the market indexes, which track the average up and down price movements of thousands of stocks listed on the various exchanges. These indexes serve as barometers of conditions in the market, and in the economy as a whole. Traders watch them religiously, using them as a basis for what and when to buy and sell, rather than holding their fingers up to the wind.

Each index consists of the group of actively traded stocks it considers to be most representative of the market, or of a particular industry or sector, in serving as economic bellwethers of market conditions.

The Major Indexes

The Dow Jones Industrial Average (DJIA)

Established in 1884 by entrepreneur Charles H. Dow, whose early financial newsletters, put out with partners Edward D. Jones and Charles M. Bergstresser under the Dow, Jones and Company banner, evolved into the *Wall Street Journal*, the DJIA is the oldest of the market indexes. It is also the most avidly scrutinized (by myself included).

Initially, it consisted of just eleven stocks, most of them transportation stocks—nine of them railroads, the blue chips of the day. By 1928, the number of blue chips included in the DJIA had expanded to thirty. It has sustained that number to this day; only the component stocks change from time to time, never the total.

The DJIA became a price-weighted index when its component stocks were upped to thirty, and it still is. Averages are arrived at by adding up the prices of all the stocks, then dividing by the number of components. But over the years, adjustments have been made to allow for stock splits, mergers, and substitutions within the Dow that could distort the index. The divisor is adjusted whenever an event occurs that could cause a distortion of ten or more points on the average. Today, the divisor is down to a little less than one. For the sake of example, let's say it's 0.345 as of this writing; here's how the formula would work:

$$\text{Sum price of all 30 shares} \div 30 \text{ components} \div 0.345 = \text{DJIA}$$

Price-weighted means that the price of an expensive Dow 30 stock has a greater influence on the average than a cheaper Dow 30 stock, even if both are moving the same number of percentage points up or down. Many market analysts believe that, in addition to the Dow's focusing too heavily on the bluest of the blue chips as market indicators, this is the DJIA's major shortcoming. They feel that, in an extreme case, the DJIA's price-weighted average could cause a misleading indication of market trends. For example, heavy momentum on the part of a few high-priced Dow components could send the average soaring in one direction while the majority of Dow components go the opposite direction, one that perhaps more accurately reflects trends in the broader market. Maybe so.

Nevertheless, I feel that when speculating in stocks, there is a tremendous advantage to limiting one's choices to the components of the Dow, particularly for the amateur investor. It is a universe of extremely liquid stocks that is easily analyzed and understood, there is enough variety to allow a sufficient degree of diversification, and they have a proven ability to survive crises and recover.

Standard & Poor's 500 Index

Established in 1923, this is the second most closely followed and widely quoted of the major indexes. It tracks four hundred industrial, sixty transportation and utility, and forty financial stocks listed on the NYSE, AMEX, and NASDAQ boards whose issuers are seen as leaders, not necessarily in price or sales perhaps, but in the industries most vital to the American economy.

Most of them are large companies, but some small companies

are included as well. Therefore, many equity observers feel the S&P 500 is a more accurate gauge of broader market performance and trends than the blue chip components of the Dow.

Unlike the Dow, the S&P is weighted according to the market value (capitalization) of its component stocks rather than price. (With the Dow, weight is proportionate to price.) This tends to give the bigger companies in the S&P, those with higher total market value, more clout than the smaller caps in influencing averages, which some see as a shortcoming, too. But the fact is, regardless of which weighting method is used, it doesn't make much of a difference under normal market conditions, as the movement of averages on the Dow and S&P tend to parallel each other.

The S&P is calculated by multiplying the stock price of each component by the number of shares outstanding, then dividing the result by the total market value of all S&P stocks from the designated base period of 1941 to 1943, and multiplying by 10.

Standard & Poor's also has two other indexes. The S&P 400 tracks the performance of four hundred medium-sized companies with a median market cap of around $1 million. The S&P 600 tracks the stocks of six hundred small companies with a median market cap above $300 million, most of which are traded on the NASDAQ. However, neither of these indexes is as widely used or quoted by the financial press and broadcast media, or as esteemed as their more important big brother.

The NASDAQ Composite Index

Established in 1971 with a base value of 100, which it still relates its average to, this market-weighted index tracks the performance of over-the-counter stocks actively traded on the NASDAQ National Market and Small Cap Market boards.

Its composition reflects the NASDAQ itself—predominantly small up-and-coming or start-up companies here and abroad, with some giants that are also listed on the bigger boards, like Microsoft (which launched itself on the NASDAQ), thrown in for good measure. Averages are thus considered to be most representative of trend line activity in the broader, more speculative small cap market.

Other Popular Indexes

The Value Line Composite Index

A source of abundant data like the S&P, but reflecting the performance of seventeen hundred NYSE, AMEX, and over-the-counter stocks more characteristic of the types of issues most small investors tend to have in their portfolios, this index was established in 1961, and uses a baseline of 100 also.

It is an equal-weighted rather than price- or market value–weighted index, meaning that each of the seventeen hundred stocks is given equal weight in determining averages, regardless of market price or total market value, so that the larger companies represented don't have a disproportionate influence on the outcome over smaller ones. It's therefore viewed as a more precise barometer of average investor feelings about the market, since its egalitarian makeup and method of measurement are more in line with the buying sympathies of that particular constituency.

The Wilshire Quality 5000 Index

Launched in 1970 by Wilshire Associates, a financial consulting firm headquartered in Los Angeles, this index is the broadest of all, tracking the movements of every domestic stock listed on the NYSE, AMEX, and NASDAQ boards, large, small, and in-between—almost seven thousand of them now, though the number it began with is still retained in its moniker. Like the S&P 500 and NASDAQ Composite Indexes, its averages are market value–weighted.

The New York Stock Exchange Composite Index

Market value–weighted also, this index measures the flow of every stock traded on the Big Board.

The American Stock Exchange Composite Index

Composed of all stocks traded on the AMEX board, this index recently replaced the American Stock Exchange Market Value Index, which had been calculated on a total returns (dividend earnings plus reinvested dividends) basis, and is now price-appreciated, market value–weighted.

Why Invest in Stocks?

In the final analysis, it comes down to this. The thing we have forgotten in this country is that every investment option is either attractive or unattractive depending on its price. *You can pay too much for stocks.* But when bought at a reasonable—and preferably cheap—price, and when bought by those who have the financial staying power to withstand the inherent volatility of the stock market, stocks, particularly the Dow 30 blue chips, have proven without a doubt to be the most profitable of the liquid investment options over time.

PART 2

Risk and Reward
Don't Always Go Together

FIVE

Stocks Are Risky

THE **GROWING BODY** of research data on investor psychology and the psychological characteristics that lead to investment success indicate, not surprisingly, that the average investor is *risk-averse*.

Researchers have even quantified the average investor's degree of risk-aversion, theorizing that for the vast majority of such people, the pain of investment loss is roughly three times greater than the joy of gain.

How do these findings square with the current stock market mania? Logic suggests that that today's equity-only advocates are unaware of the risks they're taking by placing the bulk of their hard-earned savings into investments once considered the exclusive province of gamblers, speculators, and the rich.

Add Finitum

The only risk about the stock market you hear spoken of today, particularly among average investors, is the risk of *not being in it*.

Popular expression of this belief reached a crescendo when the market hit 9000 for the first time in history on April 6, 1998, and then broke above that mark the next day.

I was watching the coverage of this watershed event in American financial history on the nightly news of one of the big three networks—each of which now devotes almost as much air-time each night to stories about the stock market as it does to the latest Washington scandals. This is a reflection of how much Main Street America's interest in (obsession with?) the stock market has grown over the years, for coverage aimed at that cherished demographic, not only by the major networks but all the print and broadcast media, has grown exponentially with it.

Moments into the story, some members of the general public were asked their reactions to the landmark 9000 breakthrough. The consensus among the few who weren't in the market yet was that it was time to get off their butts and start buying stocks; and among those already investing, that it was time to add to their shareholdings. When asked how much he really knew about stocks, one fellow quipped, "Not a lot—just enough to be dangerous." I'm sure he didn't mean it this way, but the clearest danger he represents is to himself.

The major reason for the stock market's continual climb skyward, even after it reached what then was thought to be the outer limits of valuation at the end of 1993, has been the entrance into the market of a new breed of stock investor typified by this fellow—the average Joe, or Jane, who's been putting his or her 401(k) and IRA pension plan accounts into equity mutual funds.

Prior to 1990, stocks generally were bought by knowledgeable, wealthy individual investors or pension and endowment fund managers. They understood the risks and rewards inherent in the stock market; they knew that when stocks were too high in price, to either sell or at least reduce their buying; and they could afford to ride any down wave for as long as that ride took. Today the stock market is almost completely dominated by mutual funds serving small, inexperienced investors who have gravitated increasingly toward stocks for several reasons. One reason is their quest for unrealistically high returns in order to reach their retirement goals because they haven't saved enough through the years—the United States has the lowest savings rate in the world, just 3 percent of its gross domestic product (GDP). Another is that they have been told by the "experts" that stocks are a sure thing if held for the long term. And the third reason is that the experience these small investors have had since they began dabbling in stocks in the early 1990s has been increasingly so rewarding.

Each year, after getting their annual 401(k) statements and seeing how much better their stock funds have been doing than their bond and money market funds, today's broader class of investors has gradually increased the percentage of its funds allotted to stocks each year to the point where, in most cases, virtually all of their money is going into stocks now. This is the fundamental reason why the market has continued to climb in spite of the fact that it keeps reaching increasingly absurd levels of overvaluation. Today's investors are basing their investment preference not on whether stocks offer good value, or whether the earnings of the underlying companies are growing rapidly, but almost exclusively on the theory that stocks go up because they've always gone up.

The period since 1990, during which—as I've previously described—90 percent of all the money ever invested in the equity mutual fund market has flowed into that market, there have been no stock market declines of any consequence, just a few fleeting swoons of less than 10 percent here and there. This means that 90 percent of today's equity-fiends have never experienced even a one-year loss, or even as much as a 10 percent short-term decline. They've been conditioned to believe that the market is immune to decline, a belief shared by many of their political leaders.

Why also would the government's commission on the long-term future of Social Security, which I mentioned in the introduction to this book, plan to "save" Social Security for the post-2029 generation by redirecting trillions of taxpayer dollars into the booming stock market?

Where were these visionaries when Social Security was created in the 1930s and the Dow was less than 1/100th of its current level of valuation? Common sense would suggest that, having missed out on the greatest market rise in history, Social Security might better wait for lower stock prices before allowing the unsuspecting public to risk its precious retirement savings in the most richly priced market in history. But the problem with common sense, as Samuel Johnson once said, is that there is so little of it around.

This is not to say that the theory of investing long-term in stocks to achieve greater growth and stability in our Social Security trust fund is harebrained per se—just that doing so now, when stocks are so expensive, is lunatic. One might better call such a proposal a "Plan for Saving Social Insecurity."

One of the reasons for the investing public's overoptimism is that professional market analysts have an inclination to put a too-positive spin on their earnings per share projections. As you'll recall from Chapter 4, stock prices fluctuate with earnings expectations. But earnings are almost as difficult to forecast as that other determinant of a stock's value, the P/E ratio—which, since it is virtually impossible to predict, analysts mainly tend to ignore. Table 5.1 illustrates what a poor record these analysts have demonstrated. It shows what an investment strategy, based on betting against the "experts" by buying the ten DJIA stocks that Wall Street analysts expected to have the lowest earnings for the coming year, would have produced from 1972 through 1989. Such a strategy would have produced total returns almost 50 percent better than the DJIA itself through the bear, bull, and sideways markets of the 1970s and 1980s.

Table 5.1

**The Ten DJIA Stocks
With the Lowest EPS Estimates**

Year	Total Return	DJIA
1973	–14.51	–13.12
1974	–10.52	–23.14
1975	39.21	44.40
1976	39.15	22.72
1977	–3.50	–12.71
1978	–1.82	2.69
1979	7.99	10.52
1980	29.48	21.41
1981	1.32	–3.40
1982	8.54	25.79
1983	55.25	25.65
1984	3.91	1.08
1985	42.96	32.78
1986	27.38	26.92
1987	–14.27	6.02
1988	20.59	15.95
1989	25.34	31.71
Cumulative	**729.35%**	**499.35%**

Nevertheless, both the proposal for using the stock market to rescue Social Security—that most sacred of all sacred cows in this country in terms of defining the term "risk-aversion"—and the willingness of so many people right now to put the bulk of their precious (and largely irreplaceable) life savings into stocks, bring up an interesting question. Why, in spite of their well-documented risk-aversion, are investors so increasingly inclined to invest heavily in equities?

The obvious answer is that most people today simply don't believe that stock investing is a risky business anymore, a belief substantiated by a recent Gallup poll of equity mutual fund investors. They were asked if they expected the stock market, which has been giving off returns of 20 percent per annum in the last fifteen years (the best fifteen-year run since 1817!), to do as well, better, or worse in the next fifteen years. Eighty-five percent said they expected the market to equal or better its recent fifteen-year performance.

Any student of stock market history, such as myself, would find it very hard to validate such expectations—by virtue of the fact that stocks, like trees, do not grow to the skies, not even the tallest and sturdiest redwoods among them.

Just crunch the numbers, says financial observer Allen Sloan in *Newsweek*: "The Dow [has risen] about 1,050 percent in a bit under 16 years. Say you expect this rate to continue, and you'll see this means the Dow will break the 100,000 level in December of the year 2013. If you expect the last two years' returns of about 32 percent annually to continue, the Dow will break 100,000 in less than a decade. You expect either of these things to happen? I don't."

Me neither.

Overall Market Risk

Popular wisdom suggests that since the stock market has undergone so many changes in the past several decades, historical market comparisons further back than 1970 are irrelevant to today.

These changes include: the tremendous growth of productivity-enhancing technology, the growth of international trade, institutional stock market domination that emphasizes the solid blue chips, deregulation of brokerage commissions, derivative instruments like index futures and index options, the domination of OPEC, floating exchange rates—and most important, the emergence of a new breed of small investor who will continue to "buy the dips" and hold stocks regardless of how overvalued they get or how severely the market declines in the next (and believe me, there will be a next) bear market.

Time will tell, but as a contrarian, I believe it pays to go against prevailing wisdom and take the opposing view from time to time—especially times like these when there is such extreme unanimity of opinion. Occasionally, the past has served as prologue, but as far as investor psychology is concerned, the more things have changed, the more they've remained the same. It has paid very well indeed to avoid investments that have become overly popular, such as U.S stocks in the 1920s, 1960s, and 1990s, bonds from the 1930s to the 1960s, gold and commodities in the 1970s, and real estate in the 1980s.

The basic human forces of greed, fear, and risk-aversion that inform and determine investor psychology, causing the extremes that have defined market highs and lows over the years, are still very much with us. It is this psychology, along with such "real" factors as corporate earnings and interest rates, that has and will continue to determine share prices and market direction. This is why stocks are sometimes priced to yield almost 17 percent (a price/earnings ratio, or P/E, of 6) and at other times only 3.5 percent (a P/E of 28.5).

In the almost one hundred years since 1899, we've experienced a decline in the market four out of every ten years, or about 40 percent of the time (see Table 5.2). Just in the past thirty-seven years since 1961, we've had eight major declines averaging over 30 percent. Until the 1990s, the longest-running bull market we'd had in this country stretched five years, 1924 to 1928, the period leading up to that Black Tuesday in October 1929 called the Great Crash, which sank us into the Great Depression.

According to historian Paul Sann's assessment of the prevailing wisdom of that earlier stock market era in his book *The Lawless Decade*, it was a time when "stocks only went one way—UP—and there was no reason why they shouldn't keep going that way." The similarly viewed longevity and direction of our current bull market, now almost sixteen years old and boasting an uninterrupted stretch of growth of seven years (and counting), shows just how unparalleled it is in our country's history in that single respect only.

Table 5.2
Market Declines 1899–1990

High Price	High Date	Low Price	Low Date	Percent Decline
2999.75	7/16/90	2365.10	10/11/90	–21.2%
2722.42	8/25/87	1738.74	10/19/87	–36.1%
1024.05	4/27/81	776.92	8/12/82	–24.1%
1014.79	9/21/76	742.12	2/28/78	–26.1%
1051.70	1/11/73	577.60	12/6/74	–45.1%
985.21	12/3/68	631.16	5/26/70	–35.9%
995.15	2/9/66	744.32	10/7/66	–25.2%
726.01	1/3/62	535.76	6/26/62	–26.2%
212.50	5/29/46	163.12	10/9/46	–23.2%
133.59	1/10/41	106.34	12/23/41	–20.4%
152.80	1/3/40	111.84	6/10/40	–26.8%
158.41	11/12/38	121.44	4/8/39	–23.3%
194.40	3/10/37	113.64	2/24/37	–41.5%
110.74	2/5/34	85.51	7/26/34	–22.8%
381.17	9/3/29	41.22	7/8/32	–89.2%
119.62	11/3/19	63.90	8/24/21	–46.6%
110.15	11/21/16	65.95	12/19/17	–40.1%
83.43	3/20/14	54.22	2/24/15	–35.0%
94.15	9/30/12	72.11	6/11/13	–23.4%
100.53	2/19/09	72.94	9/25/11	–27.4%
103.00	11/19/06	53.00	11/15/07	–48.5%
78.26	6/17/01	42.15	11/9/03	–46.1%
77.61	9/7/1899	52.96	9/24/1900	–31.8%

Number of Down Years 1899–1998: 35
Number of Up Years 1899–1998: 63

Unquestionably, the most egregious decline we've experienced in the market was the Great Crash of 1929–1932, where the DJIA went down almost 90 percent, conditioning a stay-away vote of no confidence that persisted with the general public for almost a generation and didn't end until the Dow exceeded its 1929 high in 1954. But let's examine the declines of more recent decades, which today's average investors, most of them baby boomers or younger, might relate to more easily than such "ancient history."

The 1960s produced two progressively longer and bigger declines, both characterized by an excessively overvalued market that saw P/E ratios pushed to then unheard-of levels. (Sound familiar?)

The fuel for overvaluation was slightly different in each case. The first run-up was characterized by an ingenuous speculation in stocks of companies in the hot new space-age and high-technology fields, many of them competitively untested and with undetermined earnings power. The second was marked by an oversold (or should I say overbought?) belief in the prowess of conglomerates to keep expanding earnings through increased diversification and acquisition, no matter how costly, plus a craze for concept stocks and other "fool's gold" opportunities. But the sputtering sound the market engine made was the same.

As earnings went unrealized, nowhere, or slipped, the market value of stocks fell to the claws of a growling bear, forcing a steep decline when investors, panicking at the sight of prices dropping, caused them to plunge even more.

The lesson unheeded, P/E ratios topped out again in the early 1970s due to a less speculative, more sober, investor game plan—put your money only in blue chip companies with steady records of growth, as earnings on these stocks could always be depended upon to keep steadily growing, even in bear markets. This theory relegated price to a position of unimportance; no matter how high stock prices climbed, you still couldn't lose, as long as you stuck with these particular stocks for the long haul. Not only could risk be averted by focusing on these four dozen or so blue chips, so the theory went, you wouldn't have to keep much of an eye on them, either. Just buy, hold, sit back and relax, easy as that. With these stocks you could afford to be Robinson Crusoe-ed on some desert island for years without ever having to sweat over how your portfolio was doing. Which is why these stocks came to be variously known as "one-decision stocks," "desert island stocks," and the "Nifty Fifty."

But escalating prices per share of these stocks fostered by rabid confidence in their predicted earnings power outstripped the capability of even the Nifty Fifty to make profits catch up to stock prices and sustain such predictions in the 1973–1974 bear market.

By the October to December period in 1974, the Dow had fallen 47 percent down to 570; twenty-seven of the Nifty Fifty, one-decision, desert islanders had fallen an average of 84 percent from their previous highs in 1972, and the group as a whole had seen earnings plummet almost 10 percent. An awful lot of people lost an awful lot of money. (See Table 5.3.)

Table 5.3

Performance of Ten "Desert Island" Stocks in the 1973–1974 Bear Market

Company	1972–73 High	1974 Low	% Decline
American Express	64.75	17.38	–73.2%
Avon Products	140.00	18.63	–86.7%
Disney	112.38	15.63	–86.1%
Honeywell	170.75	17.50	–89.8%
Howard Johnson	34.88	4.00	–88.5%
Polaroid	149.50	14.13	–90.6%
RCA	45.00	9.25	–79.4%
Simplicity Pattern	176.63	18.00	–89.8%
Westinghouse	54.88	8.00	–85.4%
Xerox	171.88	49.00	–71.5%
		Average	**–84.1%**

Market analysts next voted thumbs-up on the cyclical stocks of basic industries like steel, chemicals, aluminum, paper, and copper—profitably at first, but then the cyclicals went into another of their periodic (cyclical?) slumps. All eyes shifted toward energy stocks when oil prices soared due to the Arab oil embargo of 1973 and subsequent shortages that forced on-the-move Americans to experience the kind of rationing not seen since the days of World War II, as they sat impatiently in long lines at the gas pumps for their maximum $5 worth.

The 1970s ended and the 1980s began with America in a recession that saw energy stock prices head south. Rebounding again as America emerged from its recessionary funk in the heady Reagan era, a boom in small cap investing *a la* the 1960s led to bust when the P/Es of these stocks peaked and the market nosedived in a haze of déjà vu.

But as the Reagan administration settled into its second term and a wave of corporate takeovers, mergers, acquisitions, and buyouts by big company performers swept the landscape, along with a flood of aptly named junk bonds, optimism arose as the market settled into another "new era" of above-average averages. The figures kept going up, up, and up, setting market-expansion records as hordes of investors, many of them drawn to stocks for the first time, leaped on the bandwagon, pushing averages higher yet, with no conceivable limit in sight. This was indeed a new era, said everyone (well, almost everyone, but the naysayers were viewed as just them liberal economists up to their usual "doomspeak").

But in September of 1987, stocks began plummeting, first in the U.S. and then in overseas markets (now inexorably intertwined with our own), spreading panic here at home. Suppressed anxieties over the new frontiers of overvaluation, spiraling corporate debt, and so on were suddenly aroused. The bubble burst, with prices bottoming on Black Monday in October 1987. That 23 percent one-day decline was the fastest—and the biggest—America had experienced since that other October crash of almost sixty years earlier. It was enough

to make one heed Mark Twain's advice. "October," he wrote pre-
sciently in his 1894 novel *The Tragedy of Pudd'nhead Wilson*, "is one of
the peculiarly dangerous months to speculate in stocks." He then
added, "The others are June, July, January, September, April,
November, May, March, December, August and February."

Averages rebounded, but fell again in less spectacular fashion in
the autumn of 1990, as speculators fretted over the looming con-
frontation with Iraq following Saddam Hussein's invasion of
Kuwait. After that quick 20 percent drop, the bear entered its current long state of hibernation.

Today, the Dow is trading at almost double its historical average P/E ratio of 15. (When the Dow passed the 9000 mark, the
P/E ratio of the S&P 500 hit 28!) This means it would take a
decline of close to 50 percent just to bring today's stock market
back to average valuation levels. Not cheap levels that would
attract value investors like me, mind you. But *average levels*.

The bulk of returns of the last decade have been due to
price/earnings ratio expansion rather than substantial earnings
growth. Euphoria over the market's upward mobility has become a
self-perpetuating influence on that mobility. As economist John
Kenneth Galbraith noted in an article for *Atlantic* after the 1987
crash—and his words ring equally true of the 1929 crash, and of
conditions today: "There is a compelling vested interest in euphoria, even, or perhaps especially, when it verges, as in 1929, on
insanity. Anyone who speaks or writes on current tendencies in
financial markets should feel duly warned. There are, however,
some controlling rules in these matters, which are ignored at no
slight cost. Among those suffering the most will be those who
regard all current warnings with the greatest contempt."

As pointed out earlier, but worth repeating, not since the 1980s
have so many new investors entered the market—the largest percentage of novice speculators in history, the vast majority completely unfamiliar with what a severe market decline can cost in
psychological and economic terms.

As *Newsweek* reported in 1997: "Forty-four percent of American households now own some share of the bull market. In 1990, according to the Federal Reserve, stock holdings represented only 21 percent of households' total financial assets. By 1997, the share had doubled to 42 percent." Today, of course, those numbers are even higher.

Not knowing a price/earnings ratio from a dividend from a book value from a price to sales ratio, but having invested in the market chiefly because prices keep going up, how are these investors going to react when market prices turn around and start coming down? Even in the unusually prosperous period of the last thirty years, this has occurred almost a third of the time—not predictably perhaps, but regularly.

No one knows for sure, of course. But it seems to me that investor psychology, especially as it has revealed itself in the past, is to be ignored at one's peril as a harbinger of things to come.

In fact, we can find a reasonable indication of what's probably going to occur if we look at what's happened in Japan over the past nine years, since investor psychology, like people, tends to be much the same the world over.

In the 1980s, the mutual fund industry in Japan expanded enormously, just as it has here in the 1990s. The industry did extremely well as long as Japanese stock prices kept going up, but when the trend reversed, euphoria underwent a similar reversal, and investors began abandoning the market in droves.

The once bursting-at-the-seams Japanese economy is now possibly on the verge of entering a deflationary period of economic depression, a phenomenon resulting from a vicious circle in which falling prices lead to falling consumer spending leading to economic contraction which leads to layoffs leading to consumer pessimism which leads to higher savings and lower consumption which leads to lower prices. This same negative pattern blighted our country and the entire world in the 1920s. Unfortunately, too few of those who experienced it were around in the late 1980s to warn the Japanese, and fewer still are around today to warn us. And even if they were, who would listen to them?

As of this writing, the Japanese market has fallen more than 60 percent from the highs it reached in 1989. Mutual fund investors have continued pulling their money out of the market, leaving a virtually insignificant percentage of their assets invested in stocks at this time. Between crashing stock prices and investor withdrawals, Japanese mutual funds as a group have lost more than 90 percent of their assets over the past nine years. Investors there have shifted almost completely over to Japanese government bonds and savings accounts paying anywhere from a half of a percent to 2 percent per annum, simply because such investments pose lower risk.

This is what happens after investors get burned by the stock market—especially investors who are ill prepared economically and psychologically for a decline of any magnitude. The behavioral coin flips; true love turns to extreme hatred, an antipathy towards investing in the market that often lingers well after stocks have returned to more reasonable levels from which high returns are almost guaranteed.

For example, by 1950, eighteen years after the final market bottom in the summer of 1932, stocks were selling at 6 times earnings and dividends were 7.5 percent, while bonds were yielding 2.5 percent. Yet you couldn't give stocks away. Why? Because almost everyone alive then knew that stocks were risky, and most couldn't afford to take the risk that their savings wouldn't be available if and when needed at some point in the future. After all, stocks still hadn't returned to the prices of twenty-one years earlier, while bonds had provided steady returns of more than 4 percent a year in a period of little or no inflation. But those who bought large company stocks in 1950 compounded returns at 13.2 percent annually for the next forty-eight years. During the same period, bonds returned a meager 5.7 percent— 72 percent of which was eaten up by inflation averaging 4.1 percent.

It can take a very long time to recover losses from a major decline. As I said, if you bought stocks at the top of 1929, it was

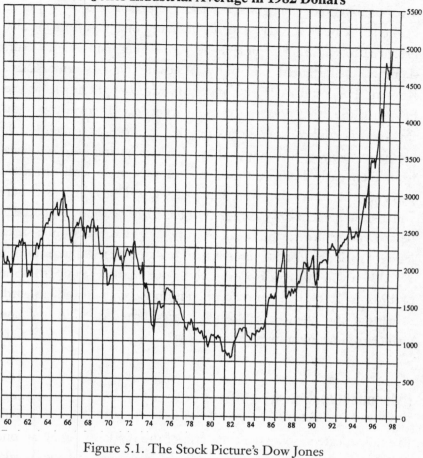

Dow Jones Industrial Average in 1982 Dollars

Figure 5.1. The Stock Picture's Dow Jones
Industrial Average 1926–1997.

The above chart shows the Dow Jones Industrial Average adjusted for inflation using 1982 dollars as the basis. This ratio provides a "deflated" DJIA, where the effects of inflation have been removed. This measure indicates to the stock investor how he would have performed in real terms. The real DJIA peaked in 1966 and declined from the late 1960s until 1982 but has been rising to date. This means that the investor in stocks would have lost ground to inflation during the 1966–1982 period but since would have achieved returns above the inflation rate.

Source: *The Business Picture.*

1959 before the Dow made a new high in real, inflation-adjusted terms. If you bought stocks in 1965, it was thirty years before the Dow made a new high in constant dollars (see Figure 5.1).

These are very long periods to wait—much longer than, investor psychology suggests, the average person who is investing in the stock market today is probably emotionally and financially prepared to endure. But unless they are willing and able to wait, there is a substantial possibility of losing big—as Indonesian, Korean, Thai, and Malaysian investors who bought stocks at the height of the 1993 boom in those markets are discovering—now that their portfolios have shrunk in value by more 90 percent!

Even today, with some of those markets having bounced back from their early 1998 bottoms, investors there are still down 80 percent from where they were four years ago. This is because when you lose 80 percent of your money, it has to go back up 400 percent before you return to the break-even point. That takes time, since it's a lot easier to lose 80 percent than it is to make 400 percent.

When you buy stocks in the midst of a market mania like that of 1982 to 1998, where no consideration is given to fundamental valuation, the chances of losing money are very high and the chances of making money are very low.

Individual Stock Risk

I've talked extensively about the risk of the market in general, but individual stocks pose greater risk because they are inherently more vulnerable to the competitive pressures and daily vicissitudes of profit and loss faced by issuers in today's global economic jungle.

A diversified portfolio helps to reduce such risk, but there are a great number of companies, including Dow components, whose stocks can suffer a significant decline in a given year—even if the market is chugging full steam ahead the same year.

This has been true of today's big bull market as well. For example, despite the DJIA's having continued soaring to all-time peaks, more than half of its components experienced severe declines during the six-month period of August 6, 1997 to February 23, 1998 before heading up again (see Table 5.4). This is a perfect example of how risky individual stocks can be—even the strongest of the strong—and how easy it is to lose money with them not just when the overall market is bad, but when it's good!

Table 5.4

Dow Downs in Today's Bull Market

Dow Component	**Close 8/6/97**	**Close 2/23/98**	**% Change**
Alcoa	$87\frac{15}{16}$	$70\frac{3}{4}$	–19.55%
AlliedSignal	$46\frac{11}{32}$	$42\frac{1}{16}$	–9.24%
American Express	$84\frac{7}{16}$	$88\frac{3}{4}$	5.11%
AT&T	$39\frac{1}{16}$	$62\frac{3}{4}$	60.64%
Boeing	$58\frac{5}{16}$	$50\frac{11}{16}$	–13.08%
Caterpillar	$58\frac{1}{2}$	$52\frac{1}{16}$	–11.00%
Chevron	$80\frac{3}{16}$	77	–3.98%
Coca-Cola	$68\frac{3}{16}$	$69\frac{3}{16}$	1.47%
Disney	$80\frac{13}{16}$	$114\frac{1}{16}$	41.14%
du Pont	$68\frac{3}{4}$	$59\frac{3}{8}$	–13.64%
Eastman Kodak	$67\frac{15}{16}$	$65\frac{3}{8}$	–3.77%
Exxon	$64\frac{7}{8}$	$62\frac{1}{2}$	–3.66%
General Electric	$69\frac{5}{16}$	$77\frac{11}{16}$	12.08%
General Motors	$63\frac{3}{4}$	$66\frac{5}{16}$	4.02%
Goodyear	$64\frac{3}{4}$	$68\frac{7}{8}$	6.37%
Hewlett-Packard	$70\frac{3}{8}$	$64\frac{3}{8}$	–8.53%
IBM	$107\frac{7}{8}$	$102\frac{7}{8}$	–4.63%
Int'l Paper	$57\frac{9}{16}$	$47\frac{1}{2}$	–17.48%
Johnson & Johnson	$62\frac{1}{4}$	72	15.66%
J.P. Morgan	$115\frac{3}{1}$	$112\frac{5}{16}$	–2.50%
Merck	102	$130\frac{5}{8}$	28.06%
McDonald's	$52\frac{3}{8}$	$52\frac{7}{8}$	0.95%
Minnesota Mining	$95\frac{7}{8}$	86	–10.30%

Dow Component	Table 5.4 (cont.) Close 8/6/97	Close 2/23/98	% Change
Philip Morris	45⁵⁄₁₆	41⁵⁄₁₆	–9.33%
Procter & Gamble	74⅜	83¹¹⁄₁₆	12.52%
Sears Roebuck	64¹¹⁄₁₆	55⅛	–14.78%
Travelers	26⅔	55⅝	19.20%
Union Carbide	56¼	46⅜	–17.56%
United Technologies	84¹⁵⁄₁₆	85¹³⁄₁₆	1.03%
Wal-Mart	38⅜	46⁵⁄₁₆	20.36%
DJIA	**8259.31**	**8410.21**	**1.83%**

There are occasions, too, where once-strong or upcoming stocks, particularly those on the broader indexes of the S&P 500 and smaller-cap NASDAQ, simply up and disappear when their issuers go bankrupt or out of business. When this happens, assets left over from liquidation are dispersed first to the company's creditors and last to holders of common stock. This is because there usually aren't enough assets left over to pay off even those first in line—the company's creditors. Shareholders are thus left out in the cold, having received absolutely nothing for the premium risk they've taken.

As a general rule, the Dow components are intrinsically less vulnerable to such horror stories. They are selected by the editors of *The Wall Street Journal* based on enormous market value, position of leadership in a particular industry or sector, consistent earnings and dividends, and most important of all, financial strength—in other words, their proven ability *not* to disappear. In fact, many components of the original Dow 30, such as General Electric, General Motors, Sears Roebuck, and Union Carbide, remain members of that elite clan today for all the above reasons.

Nevertheless, the Dow has undergone numerous deletions and substitutions over the years as companies with larger capitalization and marketplace strength have come forth, from mergers or by other means, to edge others off the list. There have been several notable such occurrences since the publication of *Beating the Dow* (see Chapter 11). But Dow component muscle is measured by degree; typically, replaced companies remain major players in their industries or market sectors. One, IBM, even returned to the list in 1979 after a forty-year hiatus.

But every rule exists to be broken; even the mighty Dow has occasionally witnessed a vanishing act performed by one of its member components.

For example, Anaconda Company, the U.S.'s leading producer of copper and aluminum, had joined the Dow in 1959, replacing American Smelting as that cyclical, highly volatile industry's leader. By 1975, Anaconda had suffered an 80 percent decline in the value of its stock, prompting its removal from the Dow. Projected to recover, Anaconda was acquired by Atlantic-Richfield (ARCO) in a 1976 takeover. But the recovery never materialized, and ARCO eventually phased this former-powerhouse-turned-struggling-subsidiary out of existence entirely.

The story of the Manville Corporation (formerly Johns-Manville), the world's largest producer of asbestos and a Dow component since the 1930s, is no less dramatic. Though it hasn't disappeared, it is today but a shadow of its former self.

Mounting lawsuits stemming from the discovery in the 1960s of the lethal effects of asbestos had driven the company's stock below the $20 a share mark by 1977, a fall of almost 87 percent from a one-time high of $150 a share. The company was forced into bankruptcy by 1982, and was deleted from the Dow the same year. By 1991, heavily restructured and having shifted to different, safer product lines such as fiberglass and plywood, Manville still faced billions of dollars in existing and potential lawsuits from the asbestos years, liabilities that far outstripped its assets. Manville stock was floating around $10 a share, and bankruptcy was an imminent prospect yet again.

These tales should serve as chilling reminders of how risky even the individual stocks of large companies—including those of the Dow—can be, given the right (or should I say wrong?) set of wholly unpredictable circumstances.

Most of the long-term studies of the market from 1925 to today that support the view that stocks are *always* the best place to be are predicated upon the idea that the chances of recovering one's losses in a major decline grow over time. As the market *always* comes back, the investor's particular stock will *always* come back too. So if, as these studies maintain, investors are willing to wait, say, just five years to recover their losses, their chances of ending up in the red at the end of that time shrink to roughly 10 percent. And if they're willing to wait up to fifteen years, their chances of ending up in the red shrink to almost zero.

But this assumes that investors haven't bought stock in a company that goes bankrupt or disappears during the waiting period, which, as I've shown, can happen even with some of the Dow heavy hitters and has occurred many times with other stocks, too. Remember the mighty Penn Central Railroad or the ubiquitous stores of W.T. Grant? So, even though the general market may recover, that particular company is no longer around to enjoy it; the stock is gone with the wind, and the investor's money along with it!

These studies supporting the five- to fifteen-year cap for back-in-the-black returns also assume the reinvestment of dividends—that investors not only hold on to their stock for the recovery period, but continue to buy more shares at a steady rate. Knowing investor psychology as I do, I doubt that most of today's neophyte stockholders will continue to reinvest their dividends if the stock market drops and stays down for a number of years or decades. Besides, most companies issuing stocks today do not have dividend reinvestment plans; investors must take their dividends. Of course, they can use their dividends to buy more shares on their own from a broker, but the purchasing power of their dividends shrinks after taxes. And when you take into account broker commission fees and other transaction costs, this too reduces the number of additional shares that can be bought—especially in a high-priced market like this one—to nurture recovery.

The bottom line is that when the market is extravagantly over-valued, stock owners are not being paid a reward anywhere near substantial enough to offset the size of the risk they're taking by owning these stocks, in the event of a major decline. Their inability to make as much increases their chances of losing more should things turn sour. And unless they can sit things out until the value of their stock recovers, and reinvest dividends to hasten the turn-around, their chances of losing even bigger goes measurably upward. This is because historically, it has been proven time after time that the waiting period is longer than most new-to-the-market stockholders (the bulk of today's investors) have the forti-tude, the bankroll, or the confidence to withstand.

That's the primary reason why, at all times, individual stock risk is greater than overall market risk—but much more so during bad economic times, or in times of panic.

Inflation Risk

The third factor that makes investing in stocks a risky business is inflation, which can be both good and bad for stocks, with hyper-inflation being *very* bad for them.

One of the major cases for owning stocks, versus T-bonds and T-bills particularly, has always been their proven ability to outpace the rate of inflation and grow in value over time. (See Chapter 4.) In fact, analysts often ballyhoo stocks as the perfect hedge against the erosion of purchasing power that inflation can pose with many other long- and short-term liquid investment vehicles. If the need arises, they say, a company can always boost the price of its prod-ucts and increase sales and profits to stay ahead of inflation and keep the market value of its stock steadily climbing, something T-bonds and T-bills intrinsically cannot do. While true enough, this only works so far, depending on how high the inflation rate soars.

Historically, inflation has seldom been much of a problem in our

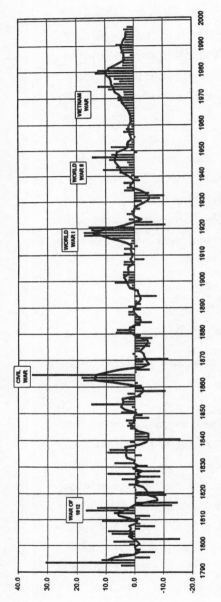

Figure 5.2. Chronological Chart of Long Term Inflation/Deflation.

A History of Long-Term Inflation Rates, 1799–1997.

- This long-term inflation portrait indicates that there has been very little deflation since the 1930s.

- The chart above shows the annual rate of change for consumer prices, which is smoothed with a five-year centered average. Assuming 1997 ends with CPI up 2.2%, this five-year average would be at 2.6%, the average of 1993–1997 annual data.

- The last deflation year for the CPI was in 1955 (−.4%), and prior to that 1949 (1.0% decline).

- But over the entire 206 year period, deflation has prevailed 35% of the time. We would caution readers to not discount the possibility of mild deflation sometimes in 1999.

- Historically, inflation has not been a permanent fixture in the U.S. economy, although since 1935, it might appear to be that way. But, if the growth in government is in fact being reined in and the budget balanced, price stability with its correcting periods of mild deflation may again prevail.

- Surges of inflation have often been associated with wars. On the chart we have noted the inflation peaks corresponding to the War of 1812, the Civil War, World War I, World War II, and the Vietnam War. The Korean War in the early 1950s did not result in surging inflation and was left off the chart, as was the Spanish American War (1848) which was more of a police action than a war.

Source: *The Leuthold Group.*

country (see Figure 5.2), but the current misperception is that it has. In fact, until double-digit inflation became common in the 1970s and early 1980s, deflation has been as great a fear as inflation. This was certainly the case from the 1930s through the 1960s when, after experiencing the deflation of the Great Depression, unemployment, not inflation, was the prime focus of our economic and political leaders. Now, in the aftermath of the inflationary '70s, these same generals are "fighting the last war" by pursuing anti-inflation policies at every turn when, in fact, the greater danger is deflation.

Until the 1970s, inflation was averaging around 2 percent (except during wartime). But it rose significantly in the early 1970s, mainly as a result of the Arab oil embargo. Shortages of home heating oil and those long lines at the gas pumps, followed by OPEC hiking the price of its crude, eventually shot domestic oil prices sky-high. This had a rippling effect throughout the U.S. economy, reflected in a huge upswing of the Consumer Price Index (CPI), the Bureau of Labor Statistics' tool for measuring changes caused by inflation in the average price of a representative sample of goods and services (food, housing, clothing, transportation) purchased by Americans. Immediately, Americans reduced their spending, thereby reducing corporate profits as well.

Out of all this came the bear market of 1973–1974, by which time inflation had reached double digits (hyperinflation), producing the sharp declines discussed earlier that saw stocks proving not so hot an inflation hedge after all. This is because when inflation gets too high, it eats away at the real returns of individual stocks, diminishing their purchasing power. In addition, the monetary authorities at the Federal Reserve Board usually try to fight the inflation by hiking interest rates enough to kill the economy and choke off the inflationary pressures. Not only does this hurt corporate profits, but the higher returns available on low-risk bonds and riskless money market instruments attract funds out of the stock market.

Inflation peaked here in the early 1980s, during a time when stock prices, triggered by a boom in small cap investing, mysteriously jumped as well, further confusing the sometimes unpredictable effect of inflation on stocks.

Nevertheless, despite this odd occurrence, the idea of controlling inflation as key to maintaining a flourishing economy has become sacrosanct. Even today, with inflation rates of below 2 percent and the bad-for-stocks prospect of deflation looming more seriously in many sectors of the economy, whenever the specter of inflation raises its ugly head—in rumor, if not actual fact—the market experiences a reactive lurch in its collective heart. Which is why, whenever the danger of inflation threatens, the Federal Reserve heads it off immediately with a moderate hike in interest rates—an action even the market (no lover of higher interest rates, just like the rest of us) has come to embrace as a necessary evil for keeping us all financially healthy.

Points to Remember

- While stocks have demonstrably proven to be superior investment vehicles longer-term, this does not alter their essential riskiness as speculative ventures.
- There have been times throughout this epic American century of ours—some quite recent—when investors lost a considerable amount of money in the stock market because they were unwise enough, or unlucky enough, to have invested their assets in stocks at points of extreme market overvaluation.
- Not only can investors suffer large declines in the value of their portfolios, but those who have the psychological and financial stamina to sit out the recovery period have often had to wait as long as twenty-five or thirty years before retrieving their losses.
- It is important—indeed critical—to know when stocks are attractive investments, relative to bonds, in terms of valuation, and how to allocate assets in a way that will provide the maximum amount of returns with the minimum amount of risk, over time.

SIX

Bonds Can Be Risky, Too

In spite of the promised return of principal and acceptable rate of interest until maturity that T-bonds provide, these supposedly "safe" investments can be far from safe at times. Investors can lose money in bonds. As history reveals in Table 6.1, there have been twenty losing years in the long-term government bond market since 1926, and nine losing years in the twenty-nine years that have gone by since 1968.*

Bonds in the Crosshairs

Bonds fluctuate widely with changes in interest rates, the inflation outlook, economic conditions, the amount of new bonds being issued, and the individual problems and circumstances affecting the many private or governmental issuers of bonds.

Of all these dangers to bonds, the most serious are any increase in the actual or expected rate of inflation, and changes in governmental

---

*However, using my new strategy presented in Part 3, eight out of those nine years could have been spent making money in the safer haven of virtually riskless T-bills (see Chapter 7, Table 7.1).

Table 6.1

Real Inflation-Adjusted Returns on
U.S. Treasury Bonds, 1926–1997

Year	Total Returns (in percent)	Inflation Rate
1926	7.77	–1.49%
1927	8.93	–2.08%
1928	0.10	–0.97%
1929	3.42	0.20%
1930	4.66	–6.03%
1931	–5.31	–9.52%
1932	16.84	–10.30%
1933	–0.07	0.51%
1934	10.03	2.03%
1935	4.98	2.99%
1936	7.52	1.21%
1937	0.23	3.10%
1938	5.53	–2.78%
1939	5.94	–0.48%
1940	6.09	0.96%
1941	0.93	9.72%
1942	3.22	9.29%
1943	2.08	3.16%
1944	2.81	2.11%
1945	10.73	2.25%
1946	–0.10	18.16%
1947	–2.62	9.01%
1948	3.40	2.71%
1949	6.45	–1.80%
1950	0.06	5.79%
1951	–3.93	5.87%
1952	1.16	0.88%
1953	3.64	0.62%
1954	7.19	–0.50%
1955	–1.29	0.37%
1956	–5.59	2.86%
1957	7.46	3.02%
1958	–6.09	1.76%
1959	–2.26	1.50%
1960	13.78	1.48%
1961	0.97	0.67%
1962	6.89	1.22%
1963	1.21	1.65%
1964	3.51	1.19%
1965	0.71	1.19%
1966	3.65	3.35%
1967	–9.18	3.04%
1968	–0.26	4.72%
1969	–5.07	6.11%
1970	12.11	5.49%
1971	13.23	3.36%
1972	5.69	3.41%
1973	–1.11	8.80%

Table 6.1 (cont.)

Year	Total Returns (in percent)	Inflation Rate
1974	4.35	12.20%
1975	9.20	7.01%
1976	16.75	4.81%
1977	−0.69	6.77%
1978	−1.18	9.03%
1979	−1.23	13.31%
1980	−3.95	12.40%
1981	1.86	8.94%
1982	40.36	3.87%
1983	0.65	3.80%
1984	15.48	3.95%
1985	30.97	3.77%
1986	24.53	1.13%
1987	−2.71	4.41%
1988	9.67	4.42%
1989	18.11	4.65%
1990	6.18	6.11%
1991	19.30	3.06%
1992	8.05	2.90%
1993	18.24	2.75%
1994	−7.77	2.67%
1995	31.67	2.54%
1996	−0.93	3.32%
1997	15.83	1.70%

Source: Ibbotson Associates.

fiscal and monetary policies. But let's look at some of the less pervasive but no less significant risks that can send bond values spiraling downward just as precipitously. I'll go into the two more mind-boggling biggies—interest rates and inflation—in greater detail later.

Leveraged Buyout (LBO) Risk

A downgrade in the quality rating of a corporation's bonds stemming from a leveraged buyout can result in huge losses for the company's bondholders. An LBO is a process by which a company is purchased using borrowed funds collateralized by the target company's assets.

There have been many egregious examples of this type of bond risk over the years, most notably during the acquisition-frenzied "greed is good" decade of the 1980s, when the volume of cash borrowed to pull off such transactions escalated from $3.1 billion a year in 1981 to $67.4 billion a year by the end of the decade.

High-Profile LBOs

RJR Nabisco

The most notorious example of the risk posed to bonds by a debt-exploding merger remains the 1988 takeover of RJR Nabisco by fellow Wall Street behemoth Kohlberg Kravis Roberts & Company (KKR) for a whopping $29.6 billion. The largest takeover deal in the history of corporate America up to that time, this cautionary tale was incisively detailed in the 1991 best-seller *Barbarians at the Gate* and hilariously (unless you were an RJR Nabisco bondholder) portrayed in a 1993 HBO movie of the same name. But I'll briefly recap the investor nightmare that transpired in my own heed-this-lesson style.

RJR Nabisco was itself the offspring of a trendsetting LBO in 1985—the $4.9 billion takeover of the National Biscuit Company (Nabisco), makers of Oreo cookies, Premium Saltines, and other fine food products, by the R.J. Reynolds Tobacco Company, creators of Camel cigarettes.

At the time of the 1988 LBO, RJR Nabisco was honchoed by the high-flying L. Ross Johnson, former CEO of Nabisco, and previous to that, head man at Nabisco competitor Standard Brands, makers of Planter's Peanuts, Blue Bonnet margarine, and other equally fine foods, a company Nabisco had absorbed in 1981.

Partnering with American Express in an endeavor to buy RJR Nabisco himself, Johnson made an enormous bid for the company in 1987, inadvertently giving a heads-up to interested, acquisition-hungry bidders elsewhere. He ran up against the equally high-flying—but in a completely terra firma, more low-profile sort of way—financier Henry Kravis, a young but old hand at the art of successfully consummating gutsy megabuck buyout deals. Johnson found that he was a baby shark in an ocean full of much bigger jaws, and he had bitten off more than he could chew. Kravis's firm already had several notches from other record-breaking buyout deals of the 1980s on its corporate belt (Gucci, probably).

Kravis capped things off with KKR's largest acquisition—and biggest notch—yet by successfully outbidding Johnson's already chart-busting offer, in a 1988 win made possible by borrowing huge amounts of cash to buy out RJR Nabisco's public shareholders. This plunged the newly restructured entity (still called RJR Nabisco) enormously into debt.

By the time the dust settled or the blood dried, whichever description you prefer, once the takeover was completed, RJR Nabisco's previously A-rated bonds had been downgraded in quality, virtually overnight, into those Michael Milken specials called junk bonds, costing RJR Nabisco's bondholders King Kong–sized losses in the value of their investment.

Texaco versus Pennzoil

No less emblematic of this boom-to-gloom kind of bond risk is the 1983–1987 saga of Texaco's bitter fight with Pennzoil over the acquisition of the Getty Oil Company, arguably financial history's most notorious ménage-à-trois.

Texas Fuel was founded in 1902 by a roughneck former oil prospector for Standard Oil named Joseph Cullinan (whose oil biz pals nicknamed him "Buckskin Joe"). It was rechristened the Texas Company in the 1930s, by which time it had become a solid Dow stock with plentiful gushers, not just in its oil-rich home state, but in Louisiana and Saudi Arabia as well. By the end of World War II, it was America's biggest and most lucrative oil company, and the only one to have service stations in all forty-eight states of the union.

Being *the* top Texas oil company, it rechristened itself again in 1959, this time as Texaco, an acronym reflecting its exalted status among Texas oil producers and its equally exalted corporate self-image. Ironically, it was shortly after the company assumed this high-toned new moniker that its fortunes began to decline due to a series of bad breaks and poor management decisions. Its domestic oil wells began drying up. Its overseas sources of crude were cut off as suppliers became nationalized and began raising prices. Yet when opportunities arose for replenishing Texaco's depleting reserves by investing in offshore exploration, particularly in oil-rich Alaska, the company's fiscally conservative and shortsighted top-down management's vote was a wrongheaded no.

By the close of the 1970s, Texaco had lost its lofty position as the nation's leading oil producer, prompting a change of management in the early 1980s whose challenge was to find a ready new source of oil and turn the company's fortunes around.

By then, America was in the grip of merger mania. Looking around for an oil-rich company it could buy, the eyes of Texaco landed on the Getty Oil Company, a relatively obscure biggie with huge oil reserves. Fortuitously, Getty Oil was shopping around just as hard for a buyer. But as in a good film noir, the flow of events now gets a bit tangled, requiring a brief flashback to bring them up to speed.

It seems Getty was looking so assiduously for a buyer that it had already landed one, a prosperous and highly ambitious oil producer called Pennzoil, Inc., with whom Getty had entered into a buyout agreement before Texaco came forward. Approved by Getty's board of directors and signed on the dotted line, the buyout agreement was considered a done deal as far as Pennzoil was concerned.

Nevertheless, Getty spread the word through the Wall Street mergers and acquisitions grapevine that it would entertain a better offer than Pennzoil's if one came forth. One did. Enter Texaco, and fade out flashback.

Though aware of the Pennzoil "done deal" and initially reluctant to horn in on it—but still mighty hungry for those rich Getty reserves—Texaco decided to go ahead; it bettered the Pennzoil offer by almost 15 percent. Getty agreed, and this time the deal *was* done. But not over.

Pennzoil sued Texaco for horning in, and the case was tried on the latter's home turf. But any expectations of partiality in the Texas court on behalf of the formerly native defendant—Texaco had long since moved its headquarters to New York City—were resoundingly dispelled when the jury found in Pennzoil's favor, and Texaco was ordered to pay the plaintiff a gigantic $10.53 billion in damages.

To avoid paying the award, Texaco appealed its case but lost, then sought bankruptcy protection, which sent the value of the corporation's bonds plummeting, leaving holders of those bonds deliriously unhappy; meanwhile, dividends were suspended, too, leaving stockholders equally unhappy.

Texaco then found itself the target of an LBO by TWA chairman and corporate raider of the lost tort, Carl Icahn. The successfully resisted takeover put a lot of money in Icahn's pocket but also helped clear the air; Texaco finally decided to come to terms with Pennzoil, and agreed to settle for a still whopping but considerably less whopping $3 billion, a decision that enabled Texaco to emerge from bankruptcy by the end of the decade and begin bettering things for itself and its investors. The company has survived handsomely (as Dow blue chips tend to do), but it took a while for bondholders and buyers (not to mention stockholders and buyers) to once again "trust [their] car to the man who wears the star."

Bankruptcy and Default Risk

When the time comes to pay, if the issuer doesn't have the money to pay and seeks bankruptcy protection, or if the marketplace perceives in the interim that the issuer may default, the short-term value of the issuer's bonds falls dramatically. Bondholders forced to sell during that period can incur substantial losses.

The following examples of several notable corporate and municipal government bond market bankruptcies and potential defaults provide stark evidence of the different kinds of economic circumstances that can lead to the same ignominious result.

High-Profile Corporate Bankruptcies and Near Bankruptcies

Chrysler Corporation

One of the original Big Three automakers along with General Motors and Ford, the Chrysler Corporation began its existence as the Maxwell Motor Car Company. When the company fell into receivership in 1920, its banker guardians, believing there might still be some gas left in the company's carburetor, brought in a new man to reorganize the ailing manufacturer from the top down and pull it out of the red.

Lured away from General Motors, where he was a vice president as well as president of GM's Buick car division, the new man was Walter Chrysler; he became president of the Maxwell Motor Car Company in 1923, and renamed it after himself a year later with his introduction of the company's first new line of cars, a six-cylinder roadster that he gave his name to as well.

The company's fortunes improved so quickly and to such a degree under Walter Chrysler's leadership that by 1928 it was able to acquire Dodge and introduce two more product lines—the economy-minded Plymouth and the more luxurious DeSoto. Turned from a laughingstock into a Dow stock in just a few short years, Chrysler had sales by 1933 that were eclipsing those of Ford.

Two years later, Walter Chrysler retired—and the visionary spirit he brought to the company retired with him for quite a long time. Focusing almost exclusively on keeping costs down, Chrysler's management team introduced no new product lines, and year after year for almost the next two decades, put out the same models of its existing line of cars with no new stylistic modifications or flourishes added. As a result of this fiscal conservatism, by 1950 Chrysler had lost a considerable amount of its market share and fallen to third place among the Big Three.

Chrysler fared little better in the 1960s when it introduced a line of small cars to a buying public whose appetite was for bigger, more luxurious cars with bottomless gas tanks, then had to scramble to catch up by turning out gas guzzlers of its own.

When oil embargoes and gas shortages forced American motorists of the 1970s to become more mileage conscious, and buyer demand turned to smaller cars and imports that delivered better miles to the gallon, Chrysler responded by continuing to produce gas guzzlers, and its market share dropped some more.

In November 1973 of the 1973–1974 bear market, to help finance its operations, the company issued $200 million worth of sinking fund debenture bonds at par, paying 8 percent a year over twenty-five years. The following year, new car sales of all the domestic automakers nosedived 20 percent, but Chrysler's income suffered the most. Losses escalated each year thereafter, reaching more than $1 billion in 1979 and 1980. Replaced on the Dow by International Business Machines (IBM), the company faced bankruptcy by mid-1980, its bonds trading that summer as low as 28 cents on the dollar.

Then Lee Iacocca, a maverick in the Walter Chrysler tradition, came to the rescue, along with Uncle Sam. Iacocca was the former president of Ford Motor Company, where he had spearheaded development of the popular Mustang. He actually had joined the fray two years earlier, when Ford fired him and he jumped aboard the crumbling Chrysler as new CEO.

With the American economy deep in recession by mid-1980 due to rising interest rates and worsening inflation, Iacocca hoped that the federal government wouldn't want to aggravate the country's economic woes in an election year by allowing Chrysler, a major defense contractor with 100,000 employees, to go under. So he appealed to the Carter administration for help. His request for

$1.5 billion in loan guarantees ignited a firestorm of controversy on Capitol Hill over the role of government in a market economy; but the persuasive Iacocca got his way, and Congress finally agreed to cough up the loans, provided that Chrysler came up with an additional $2 billion on its own.

Iaccoca accomplished this feat by downsizing operations, closing plants, successfully prevailing upon the labor unions to go along with wage cuts and layoffs, and changing the company's product line focus from gas guzzlers to smaller, more fuel-efficient cars. He appeared on television almost as frequently as the two candidates in the upcoming presidential election of 1980, Carter and Reagan. Iacocca became the most visible and well-known CEO in history up to that time, as he personally huckstered Chrysler's new line of better-mileage K-cars to the public in expensive prime time.

The company showed a small profit in 1981, but by 1983 was more than $2 billion in the black. Iacocca's leadership and hucksterism had paid off. The government's loans were fully paid back that same year, seven years ahead of schedule. And the era of CEO-as-media-superstar was ushered in.

Though Iacocca retired as head of Chrysler in 1992, the company has continued to thrive. But until Uncle Sam stepped in to bail Chrysler out, investors who had bought the company's bonds back in 1973 were earning negative annual current interest of minus 3.1 percent (an 8 percent coupon minus 9.3 percent average inflation). And those who panicked and sold their bonds before the mid-1980 bailout lost 72 percent of their principal.

W.T. Grant

A pioneer in the discount department store business, along with Woolworth's and other retailers, W.T. Grant Company opened the first of its "five-and-dime" outlets in 1906, specializing in variety goods as well as apparel and home furnishings. Advertising itself as the company "known for values," it expanded its line of general merchandise to include discounted bigger ticket items like home appliances, and eventually grew into the ninth-largest retailer in America, with stores in the major cities of all fifty states and annual sales in excess of $1.8 billion.

But then Murphy's Law befell the company; everything that could go wrong did, at the worst possible time.

W.T. Grant began to face stiff competition from other discounters that had begun to diversify away from downtown locations, which were becoming increasingly moribund, into America's suburbs and rapidly growing number of shopping malls. The company initially responded by expanding its credit sales operations as a way to attract more customers, rather than joining the exodus to the 'burbs. Continuing to feel the competitive pinch, however, the chain finally realized it not only had to expand its reach into nonurban areas like everybody else, but had to do so quickly. Seeking loans to finance the expansion, in 1962 the company issued a huge volume of 4.75 percent sinking fund debentures (due January 1987) at par.

The company began opening new stores across the country in record numbers in record time—an astonishing 376 of them alone between 1969 and 1973. However, as the company was playing a game of catch-up, a lot of the choicer venues were already taken; many of Grant's new sites were either in poor locations, leased at inflated rates, or both.

As a result of the hyperexpansion, and the need to borrow more money to buy more inventory, the chain's debt by 1973 had exploded to more than $1 billion—just at the time when the economy was slipping into recession due to higher interest rates and high inflation. Grant's sales did a bungee jump without the cord. The volume of unsold inventory mounted. And the volume of customer credit sales that went unpaid (and uncollectable) increased as well.

In a last gasp to stanch the flow of its corporate blood, which was refusing to congeal, the chain shuttered the windows on 126 of its 1,194 outlets, reduced its workforce by almost 20 percent, cut customer credit sales sharply, and requested its unpaid suppliers to keep delivering goods on faith and credit until the above measures turned things around. Some agreed to; most didn't.

Alas, that chance never came. By 1975, it had become clear to everyone, especially W.T. Grant, that these measures weren't working—not fast enough, anyway—and the venerable retailing giant was forced to enter bankruptcy proceedings. It was the second-largest failure of a U.S. company in the history of American business up to that time. The 1970 collapse of Penn Central Railroad claimed the dubious honor of holding the top spot.

More than $300 million of the company's outstanding debts were written off as a loss by its twenty-seven bank creditors. This put the company between a rock and a hard place by reducing its chances of borrowing more money to climb out of bankruptcy from slim to none. The old-line retailing giant went down for the count.

The impact on bondholders was this: At the bond market bottom in 1974, the bonds that investors had bought back in 1962 were trading as low as $20. The following year, just before the company went bankrupt, they'd sunk to $15. During that thirteen-year period between 1962 and 1975, bondholders who'd bought those bonds were being paid 4.75 percent annually when inflation averaged 4.5 percent—a meager 0.25 percent return in real current interest. Then they *lost* almost all of their principal when W.T. Grant went belly-up.

High-Profile Local Government Bankruptcies

The New York City Financial Crisis

"Welcome to Fear City!" screamed the grim reaper from the covers of thousands of leaflets flooding the streets of the Big Apple during the long, hot summer of 1975.

Inside the four-page leaflets, subtitled "A Survival Guide for

Visitors to the City of NY," big, bold text warned tourists to self-impose a curfew and stay indoors after the sun went down for their own protection, to shun public transportation—especially those deep, dark, scary New York subways; and if they had any sense, to avoid coming to New York in the first place "until things improve."

It was bad enough that *Death Wish*, the Charles Bronson movie released the year before about a mild-mannered businessman who turns vigilante in order to rid the Big Apple of omnipresent thugs, had already made out-of-towners overly nervous about putting their lives in jeopardy to catch a Broadway show. Now here were the city's own public employee unions (the publishers and distributors of the leaflets), scaring the hell out of potential tourists, whose dollars the city counted on. How had things gotten so badly out of hand?

Though the seeds of all the trouble were sown much earlier during previous administrations, the situation reached its boiling point when the city's newest mayor, Abraham Beame, a former accountant turned civil servant, had taken a number of extreme measures to lift the city out of the economic woes he'd inherited upon taking office. In spite of strong opposition from the city's public employee unions, he'd laid off four thousand workers. He'd reduced police, fire, and sanitation services. He'd increased teachers' workloads. He'd pressured the city's men in blue to patrol the streets for a year without salary. And he'd raised the city's real estate taxes 10 percent, to the chagrin of business owners and citizens alike.

The dire financial straits that necessitated such actions included a city budget that was already more than $100 million in the red, and a nationwide recession coupled with high inflation, whose impact on the local economy had reduced city tax collections by $150 million while causing city expenditures to soar to an astronomical $12.5 billion. Furthermore, the city's long-standing practice of borrowing money to meet the payroll by issuing more and more public debt—which now topped $13.7 billion in outstanding notes and bonds—had run smack into a dead end.

The eleven major banks underwriting the city's debt obligations had put their collective foot down and ceased competitive bidding on any more issues until the city got its financial house in order, just as scores of the city's existing issues were reaching maturity and payment was finally coming due to anxious investors. Moreover, Moody's Investment Service had downgraded the quality rating of the city's bonds from A to Ba, a change that would likely cost the city millions of dollars more in high interest. With the city in a state of bankruptcy and technical default, the already gray-haired Abe Beame probably wished he hadn't gotten elected.

As the city's financial travails had been caused in no small part by the many payroll-hiking concessions that previous administrations had made to its municipal employee, teacher, and police unions over the years, Beame now sought payroll-reducing concessions of his own from these same unions in an effort to ease the budget burden. He succeeded in getting a few, but union opposition to most of his demands was so strong that he was forced to brazen it out and take the extreme measures mentioned earlier.

The unions' anticipated wrath resulted in those unanticipated scare-tactic leaflets. The administration had to seek a court order to get these materials permanently off the street before even more tourists were scared away. In a backlash against the unions' pamphleteering, many of their own members protested against the leaflets as well, feeling the "shun New York" hyperbole was hardly conducive to their own personal and financial well-being.

But the major problems of bankruptcy and potential default remained. The city turned to Washington for help. But the Ford administration opposed federal assistance, even though Federal Reserve Chairman Arthur Burns cautioned that, with the country finally beginning to show signs of climbing out of recession, the New York City fiscal crisis could severely injure the recovery process now under way in our national economy. Slowly, some members of Congress began to listen. But in the meantime, the

State of New York rushed in and came to the city's aid of its own accord. It created a new agency, the Municipal Assistance Corporation (or "Big Mac" as it was soon called, perhaps in a nod to fast-food America's heartiest meal).

Big Mac's mission was to pull the Big Apple back from the brink by converting $3 billion of the city's short-term notes into long-term bonds. Although far inferior pieces of paper in terms of compensation, they were better than nothing to investors who were not getting paid at all.

To make a long and convoluted tale short, the bailout strategy—assisted by some federal aid that finally did come—ultimately succeeded in getting the city's fiscal problems under control and keeping them there. But until things got better, they often got worse; there were times during the city's pullback from financial collapse when its Big Mac bond prices went down in value as low as 75 cents on the dollar.

The Orange County Fiscal Crisis

One of the wealthiest per capita income areas in the state, Orange County was, like every other California local government, bound by strict new laws that put constraints on its ability to raise revenues and reduce expenditures.

On the one hand, California's tough Proposition 13, for which the majority of Orange County residents had enthusiastically voted, limited the power of all statewide local governments to raise taxes to pay for municipal programs and services. On the other hand, the Sacramento legislature had imposed statewide mandates on local governments to implement many programs and services, particularly in the health and social services (i.e., welfare) area.

Confronted by the double-edged sword of seeing its revenues reduced and the simultaneous need to meet rising expenditures, the Orange County municipal government sought an alternative money stream from higher-yielding, higher-risk investments to help ease the strain on its budget. However, rising interest rates in

1994 resulted in a huge $1.7 billion loss in the market value of the county's investment portfolio. As the situation became clear to the portfolio's pool of investor participants, which included two hundred government entities in and out of the county as well as note and bondholders, many of them tried to withdraw their funds. This created a liquidity crisis the portfolio couldn't withstand; Orange County was forced to file for Chapter 9 protection under the Federal Bankruptcy Code.

Other U.S. municipalities had similarly sought bankruptcy protection as a way of gaining themselves breathing room until they could bounce back; but what made this case virtually unprecedented, and sent shock waves throughout the local government bond markets across the land, was that the prospect of Orange County's defaulting on its obligations looked imminent as well. Its repayment resources devastated, the county had, according to a contemporary article in *Public Management* written by two public policy observers of the crisis and its implications, chosen "to put itself in an adversarial position with its creditors, including bondholders, [by threatening] to invalidate some of its debt obligations [i.e., pay some creditors and not others]."

By looking to apply corporate bankruptcy practices to resolve its financial woes, the county was in danger of breaching several assumptions under which the municipal bond market had long operated, the observers said. "First, that bankruptcy is an option of last resort for any local government [since] governments must continue to perform their functions even in times of fiscal distress because thousands, if not millions, of people depend upon [many essential] governmental services. And second, that even in the case of bankruptcy, repayment could still be achieved.

"If Orange County were to default on its obligations, or, even worse, actively attempted to repudiate its debt," these assumptions would no longer be deemed true and the implications could be far-reaching, the observers concluded. Creditors might be "unwilling to lend credit in the future or [would] do so [only] at a high price.

Even after emerging from bankruptcy, market penalties may persist. Only if Orange County consistently acts to avoid default will the faith on which the market operates—the belief that governments will honor their commitments—be restored."

Orange County ultimately responded by putting budgetary controls and structural changes in place that enabled it to continue performing vital services to citizens, yet still satisfy creditor concerns and address its other liabilities. It subsequently took other measures to climb out of the hole and stay out through better oversight of its investment practices, and Orange County's bonds have steadily improved in investment grade. But its almost-collapse serves as a potent warning of the risk local government bond investment can sometimes hold—even when the issuer is one of the richest municipalities in America.

Avoiding Default Risk

This can be done in a very simple way, by concentrating your bond portfolio in U.S. Treasuries, the bond market selection my new strategy points to as the investment of choice, especially for the average investor.

T-bonds are extremely liquid. By that I mean you can buy and sell them more quickly and easily than any other type of bond. This is because T-bonds are so widely issued, there are so many of them outstanding (because the U.S. government has borrowed so much over time), there are so many transactions of T-bonds in a given day, and so many dealers in them, that the spread between the bid price and the asked price on T-bonds is very low.

Typically, the spread between the bid price and the asked price on other, less liquid bonds can be often as high as 5 percent. But the spread on T-bonds is very often as low as 2/32nds, or 0.06 of a percent. In addition to the liquidity advantage, this means that overall transaction costs for investors are lower with T-bonds than with any other type of bond, another key reason for concentrating on Treasury securities, aside from the paramount one of avoiding default risk.

Interest Rate and Inflation Risk

Normally, higher interest rates cause bonds to fall in price, and lower interest rates lead to higher bond prices. However, in a generally deteriorating economy, lower-grade corporate bonds often go down in price in spite of declining rates on government bonds. The reason for this exception is that investors question the ability of weak companies to pay the principal and interest on their outstanding bonds, resulting in low-quality bond losses in a generally strong bond market.

A perfect example of this happened during the Great Crash of 1929–1932, when rates on long-term government bonds fell fairly steeply because of the oncoming Depression. But rates on Baa-rated bonds, which are not even low-grade but the lowest category of investment-grade bonds, doubled. Short-term interest rates between those years went from 5 7/8 percent to 7/8 percent, but in spite of that, Baa-rated bonds lost almost half their value. Therefore, in the face of plummeting short- and long-term interest rates during that time, investors lost close to half their capital if they'd invested in Baa-rated bonds. Imagine how much junk bond buyers lost! So, that's how the fear of severe economic weakness can pose a risk to bonds.

Another way is through higher interest rates in general; these are usually brought about by changes in inflationary expectations, which prompt skittish investors to sell some of their bond holdings or at least stop purchasing new bonds. Our nation's central bank, the Federal Reserve (a.k.a. the Fed), usually responds by increasing short-term interest rates and raising the amount that member banks must keep on deposit at the Fed, thereby reducing the money supply and raising the price of credit at the same time. So, it's not just actual inflation but inflationary *expectations* that change interest rates and damage bond values.

A perfect example of this was in 1994, when expectations of higher inflation caused the Federal Reserve to hike short-term interest rates from 3 percent to 5 percent. This, in turn, led bond market investors to dump their bond holdings, resulting in the worst bond market decline in history. But inflation never picked up. It stayed the same in 1994 as it had been 1993, approximately 2.7 percent. However, the fact that expectations were wrong didn't help bondholders much. They still lost a ton of money.

The Big Kahuna

The most common way of losing money in T-bonds is through fluctuations in interest rates, fluctuations that can sometimes last a very long time.

For example, bonds that were issued by corporations in the 1930s, 1940s, and 1950s, when interest rates were low, lost considerable value when interest rates shot up in the 1960s and 1970s due to rapidly rising inflation. Many of these bonds were selling at 50 to 60 cents on the dollar in the early 1980s. Those who had purchased these bonds back when they were issued were now sitting with a coupon of 3 to 4 percent at a time of double-digit inflation, rendering that coupon virtually meaningless.

We had fairly long periods in the 1960s, 1970s, and early 1980s when interest rates averaged 6, 7, and 8 percent for as long as ten years, and actually got as high as 15 percent in 1981. These were rates two, three, and four times the historical norm (see Figure 6.1). As a result, bonds issued when interest rates were normal got absolutely crucified when they were not. Bondholders were stuck with laughable coupons during these high-inflation years. And if they'd sold their bonds, they would have suffered a severe loss of principal, not to mention seeing the money they did make eroded by inflation. If, for example, they sold their bonds for 50 cents on the dollar, but the bonds had originally cost them 100 cents on the dollar, not only were they losing half their principal, but inflation had probably eroded the worth of that 50 cents on the dollar to 40 cents or even less. That's not the kind of loss you expect from a supposedly supersafe investment!

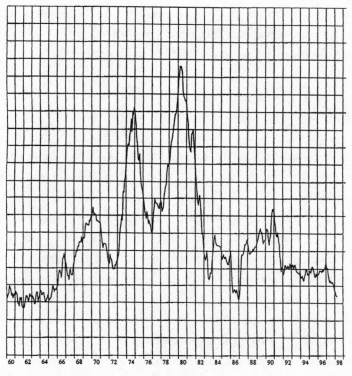

Figure 6.1. Consumer Price Index Year-to-Year Changes, 1960–1998.

The consumer price index is the most widely used measure of the cost of living in the U.S. It is a proxy for inflation at the retail level. The Bureau of Labor Statistics computes this index to measure "changes in the average price of a representative sample of goods and services purchased by typical wage earners and clerical workers in urban areas of the U.S." The major categories of the CPI are food, housing, apparel and its upkeep, transportation, and medical care. Problems with the interpretation of the CPI are: it is based only on prices found in urban areas; there are long delays in recalibrating the index to make it more responsive to changing consumer tastes; the index cannot discriminate between changes caused by inflation and those caused by changes in the quality of goods and services; and expenditure patterns of most people do not match that of the "typical" wage earner.

A look at the price sheets for T-bonds during the high-inflation years of 1974 and 1981 (see Tables 6.2 and 6.3) clearly illustrates the dangers of this type of bond risk.

At the bottom of the bond market decline in 1974, there were a large number of T-bonds selling at below 70 cents on the dollar. And at the bottom of the 1981 market, there were almost a dozen issues selling at less than 60 cents on the dollar, with not a single issue in the black. This means you would have lost 30 to 40 percent of your principal if you had been forced to sell during those years. In addition, that 60 or 70 cents wouldn't have been worth as much in real terms compared to the purchase price, due to the erosionary effects of inflation.

For example, if you were so unlucky as to have bought the 7 5/8 issue of February 15, 2007 when it was first sold, and been forced to sell at the bottom of the 1981 market, you would have gotten less than 54 cents on the dollar, and lost 46 percent of your capital.

Also, in both years, but particularly 1974, you would have been stuck with ridiculously low coupons at a time of double-digit rates of inflation.

By 1981, the size of coupons had improved somewhat because, by that time, investors had become used to the idea of inflation and were demanding higher current returns. Unfortunately, even though bonds were drawing closer to the inflation rate in terms of real interest, the rates of return, adjusted for inflation, were still on the negative side.

Table 6.2
U.S. Treasury Bonds 1974 Price Range

Many T-bonds were down over 30 percent at the 1974 bond market bottom. With coupons averaging 3.5 percent during 10.9 percent inflation, this meant investors who bought those bonds when originally issued were receiving a *negative current return* annually of minus 7.4 percent (3.5 percent minus 10.9 percent) after inflation, in addition to suffering a paper loss of 30 percent of their principal.

	High	Low	Last
4s Feb 1980	86.14	79.14	86.4
3½s Nov 1980	84.2	76.12	83.18
7s Aug 1981	102.8	93.16	99.2
6⅜s Feb 1982	97.16	87.16	94.14
3¼s Jun 1978–83	75.22	69.28	75.2
6⅜s Aug 1984	96.6	87.12	94.28
3¼s May 1985	75.16	69.26	75.2
4¼s May 1975–85	78.8	72.12	77.28
6⅛s Nov 1986	92.14	87.16	91.8
3½s Feb 1990	75.8	69.24	74.20
4¼s Aug 1987–92	75.26	70.8	75.6
4s Feb 1988–93	75.14	69.30	74.18
6¾s Feb 1993	100.22	82.18	91.0
7½s Aug 1988–93	100.30	75.20	96.16
4⅛s May 1989–94	75.22	69.26	74.28
3s Feb 1995	95.18	69.24	74.16
7s May 1993–98	96.4	84.4	92.0
3½s Nov 1998	75.0	69.24	74.12
8½s May 1994–99	105.18	97.2	103.14

Table 6.3

U.S. Treasury Bonds 1981 Price Range

Some T-bonds were down almost 50 percent at the 1981 bond market bottom. Coupons averaging 7.3 percent during 10.9 percent inflation meant that investors were receiving *negative* real interest of minus 3.6 percent after inflation.

	High	Low	Last	Net Chg
6.38 Feb 1982	99.9	92.24	99.9	+5.25%
13.00 Dec 1983	98.30	98.3	98.30	-1.70%
6.38 Aug 1984	88.4	78	84.18	+2.22%
3.25 May 1985	84.31	76.12	83.30	+2.17%
14.25 May 1975–85	85.6	73.26	84.22	+3.6%
11.75 Nov 1985	99.4	86.18	93.2	–4.18%
6.13 Nov 1986	79.22	67.18	75.10	–2.8%
3.50 Feb 1990	85.16	74.12	82.23	+1.16
8.25 May 1990	81.1	67.14	72.21	–4.10%
4.25 Aug 1987–92	85.13	73.22	84.28	+2.18%
7.25 Aug 1992	71.22	57.2	65.18	–4.10%
4.0 Feb 1988–93	85.24	75	83.12	+.16%
6.75 Feb 1993	69.25	55.8	62.14	–4.70%
7.88 Feb 1993	74.13	59	66.24	–5.26%
7.50 Aug 1988–93	73.7	57.12	64.20	–6.40%
8.63 Aug 1993	78.7	62.12	69.14	–7.40%
8.63 Nov 1993	78.8	62.12	69.10	–7.40%
9.0 Feb 1994	80.20	63.12	71.14	–7.60%
4.13 May 1989–94	84.18	74.12	82.16	+.80%
8.75 Aug 1994	78.20	62.8	69.10	–7.17%
10.13 Nov 1994	87.29	69.16	77.14	–8.10%
3.0 Feb 1995	85.22	74.16	83.10	+1.26%
10.50 Feb 1995	90.5	71.8	79.16	–8.25%
10.38 May 1995	89.5	70.10	78.12	–8.26%
12.63 May 1995	103.10	83.8	92	–9.40%

Table 6.3 (cont.)

	High	Low	Last	Net Chg
11.50 Nov 1995	96.14	76.12	84.30	−9.90%
7.0 May 1993–98	84.4	51.2	58.28	−6.40%
3.50 Nov 1998	85.20	73.22	83.14	−.15%
8.50 May 1994–99	76.28	59.20	67.4	−6.20%
7.88 Feb 1995–00	71.4	54.12	61.1	−8.30%
8.38 Aug 1995–00	74.22	55.26	64.18	−8.20%
11.75 Feb 2001	97.27	76.20	84.31	−15.03%
13.13 May 2001	102.18	84.26	93.18	−6.44%
8.0 Aug 1996–01	72.15	56.2	62.28	−7.15%
13.38 Aug 2001	103.18	86.8	95.11	−4.66%
15.75 Nov 2001	118.10	100.30	110.8	+10.25
8.25 May 2000–05	73.18	57.6	63.29	−7.23%
7.63 Feb 2002–07	69.15	53.10	59.26	−7.24%
7.88 Nov 2002–07	71.19	54.28	61.25	−8.60%
8.38 Aug 2003–08	74.22	57.18	63.30	−8.25%
8.75 Nov 2003–08	77.15	59.30	66.14	−8.28%
9.13 Nov 2004–09	80.12	62	68.31	−9.90%
10.38 Nov 2004–09	90.3	69.10	77.5	−10.27%
11.75 Feb 2005–10	100.25	78.2	86.6	−11.30%
10.0 May 2005–10	87.23	66.26	74.6	−11.70%
12.75 Nov 2005–10	108.31	84	93.18	−12.20%
13.88 May 2006–11	109.29	91.10	101.13	+1.41%
14.0 Nov 2006–11	109.16	100.28	102.17	+2.53%

The Good, the Bad, and the Ugly

The most graphic demonstration that T-bonds can sometimes be a very good investment, sometimes a very bad one, and sometimes a painfully ugly one, depending upon interest rates and the outlook for inflation during those times, is illustrated in Table 6.4. It compares real, inflation-adjusted returns on T-bonds during four different periods, from 1926 to 1940, 1941 to 1980, 1981 to the present, and since 1968.

Beginning year-end 1926 to year-end 1940, real returns on T-bonds were 6.6 percent. That was composed of a nominal return averaging 5 percent a year and a rate of deflation averaging minus 1.6 percent a year during those fourteen years.

However, if you'd bought bonds at the end of 1941 and held them until the end of 1980, you would have averaged a negative real return of minus 2.5 percent after inflation—during a time when many other types of investments, particularly stocks, did extremely well.

But in 1981, President Ronald Reagan and his Federal Reserve chairman, Paul Volcker, combined efforts to defeat inflation. We've been living with the legacy of their beneficial efforts ever since. Unlike the preceding forty-year period when bondholders lost 2.5 percent annually after inflation, bond yields since 1981 have averaged inflation-adjusted yearly returns of 10.1 percent—more than five times the long-term historical norm for high-quality bonds going all the way back to Babylonian times. And ever since 1968, when bonds first became cheaper than stocks, real returns on T-bonds have averaged 3.6 percent, almost double the historical rate of return on bonds of 2 percent a year.

Looking Ahead

In the world of bonds, zero coupon Treasury bonds offer the most appreciation opportunity.

As noted in Chapter 2, zeros don't reward you with periodic interest payments. You buy a zero coupon bond at a discount from its face value. The value of your zero coupon bond grows year by year until you are repaid at full face value when the bond matures.

Table 6.4

**U.S. Treasury Bond Bid-End
Real Return Averages,
1926–1997**

1926–1940	CPI	= –1.60%/yr.
	Bonds	= +5.02%/yr.
	Real returns	**= +6.6%/yr.**
1941–1981	CPI	= 4.70%/yr.
	Bonds	= 2.20%/yr.
	Real returns	**= –2.50%/yr.**
1982–1997	CPI	= 3.40%/yr.
	Bonds	= 13.50%/yr.
	Real returns	**= +10.10%/yr.**
Since 1968	CPI	= 5.40%/yr.
	Bonds	= 9.00%/yr.
	Real returns	**= +3.60%/yr.**

That makes zero coupon bonds highly advantageous in two ways. If long-term interest rates go up, 30-year zero coupon bonds will give you twice the return of conventional bonds. And you don't have to reinvest your interest income each year because there are no periodic interest payments.

I believe the annual return on zero coupon bonds will approach 20 percent a year for the next three years. This kind of profit potential in such relatively safe instruments is a lot better than the 40 percent to 50 percent decline I anticipate will occur in the stock market during the same period.

SEVEN

Treasury Bills:
The Ultimate Safe Haven?

THE PHRASE "no guts, no glory" would certainly apply to returns received by T-bill investors—whom we should really call *savers*, because people don't actually *invest* in T-bills. They put money in them when the need arises for a riskless, interest-bearing, comfortable old shoe.

When compared to their principal competitors, stocks and bonds, which have generated returns four to twenty times higher than T-bills over time, they may appear rather unappealing.

But, as veterans of the investment wars like me know very well, it can be deliciously profitable to hold supersafe T-bills during times when neither stocks nor bonds themselves are appealing.

In 1989, for example, while long-term T-bonds and stocks were giving investors *losses* of 5.1 percent and 8.5 percent respectively, 1-year T-bills returned 7.5 percent, well above the 6.11 percent CPI increase of that year.

Earlier, in 1973, while stocks had *negative* returns of minus 14.66 percent and bonds cost their holders 1.11 percent *before* the

Table 7.1
Real Inflation-Adjusted Returns
on U.S. T-bills, 1926–1996

Year	Total Returns (in percent)	Inflation Rate
1926	3.27	−0.49%
1927	3.12	−2.08%
1928	3.56	−0.97%
1929	4.75	0.20%
1930	2.41	−6.03%
1931	1.07	−9.52%
1932	0.96	−10.30%
1933	0.30	0.51%
1934	0.16	2.03%
1935	0.17	2.99%
1936	0.18	1.21%
1937	0.31	3.10%
1938	−0.02	−2.78%
1939	0.02	−0.48%
1940	0.00	0.96%
1941	0.06	9.72%
1942	0.27	9.29%
1943	0.35	3.16%
1944	0.33	2.11%
1945	0.33	2.25%
1946	0.35	18.26%
1947	0.50	9.01%
1948	0.81	2.71%
1949	1.10	−1.80%
1950	1.20	5.79%
1951	1.49	5.87%
1952	1.66	0.88%
1953	1.82	0.62%
1954	0.86	−0.50%
1955	1.57	0.37%
1956	2.46	2.68%
1957	3.14	3.02%
1958	1.54	1.76%
1959	2.95	1.50%
1960	2.66	1.48%
1961	2.13	0.67%
1962	2.73	1.22%
1963	3.12	1.65%
1964	3.54	1.19%
1965	3.93	1.92%
1966	4.76	3.35%
1967	4.21	3.04%
1968	5.21	4.72%
1969	6.58	6.11%
1970	6.52	5.49%
1971	4.39	3.36%

Table 7.1 (cont.)

Year	Total Returns (in percent)	Inflation Rate
1972	3.84	3.41%
1973	6.93	8.80%
1974	8.00	12.20%
1975	5.80	7.01%
1976	5.08	4.81%
1977	5.12	6.77%
1978	7.18	9.03%
1979	10.38	13.31%
1980	11.24	12.40%
1981	14.71	8.94%
1982	10.54	3.87%
1983	8.80	3.80%
1984	9.85	3.95%
1985	7.72	3.77%
1986	6.16	1.13%
1987	5.47	4.41%
1988	6.35	4.42%
1989	8.37	4.65%
1990	7.81	6.11%
1991	5.60	3.06%
1992	3.51	2.90%
1993	2.90	2.75%
1994	3.90	2.67%
1995	5.60	2.54%
1996	5.21	3.32%
1997	5.26	1.70%

inflation rate of 8.80 percent was figured in, 1-year T-bills gave their owners a 6.76 percent profit before inflation.

That's the good news about T-bills.

The bad news about them, which I exposed briefly in Chapter 3, is that there is one basic enemy of T-bills that can cause you to virtually *lose* money even in these safety-first, -last, and -always, fixed-income securities. The enemy is called the rate of inflation, which can drive up general interest rates, thereby forcing the value of T-bills down.

Defensive Action

The one exception, in this century anyway, was in the 1930s and 1940s. Inflation posed absolutely no risk to T-bills in that period, yet savers were so worried about risk that they were even willing to pay a premium for them. I touched upon this phenomenon in Chapter 3, but it's worth elaborating upon because it presents additional evidence of just how risk-averse investors can be in the wake of a major decline, and how long afterward they can remain that way.

As I pointed out in Chapter 3, T-bills are the shortest-term obligations issued by the U.S. government, with the 3-month, or 90-day, T-bill the most popular maturity among the majority of savers. They are sold at a discount from their minimum $1,000 face value, and do not pay any interest until maturity. The yield received is the difference between the discounted price paid and the 100-cents-on-the-dollar face value gotten back when the bill reaches maturity.

With the Great Crash of 1929 having thrown Americans into a panic over the security of their savings, and the Depression making cash harder and harder to come by for millions of out-of-work citizens, by 1932 a massive run on bank deposits had forced hundreds of banks across the country to close their doors forever, threatening the structure of the nation's banking system with collapse.

To shore up the banking system and prove to Americans that they had nothing to fear but fear itself, newly elected President Franklin Delano Roosevelt counterpunched by ordering a bank holiday two months after his January 1933 inauguration, then pressing Congress to enact emergency legislation that would throw the full financial force of America's Federal Reserve behind America's banks by insuring all customer deposits.

Nevertheless, despite these new safeguards and no inflation to speak of, millions of America's savers remained so nervous about the stability of the nation's banks in the wake of their Roaring

Twenties hangover that they preferred paying the U.S. government to store their money for them by buying T-bills at more than face value—in other words, for a price higher than the bills would return at maturity. This was clearly a demonstration of investor risk-aversion at its most pronounced.

But in some respects, such a move wasn't quite as illogical, or irrational, as it may now seem. The country was, to a large extent, in a state not just of no inflation but of actual deflation, which many people believed was perpetual. Therefore, they were much less concerned about enhancing principal than holding on to the money they already had and not losing it. Parking their money in the safe haven of T-bills, even for a premium parking fee, enabled them to do that.

Macro Versus Micro

While T-bills, when held to maturity, have historically provided slightly positive returns (even after inflation) over time, they've averaged about 3.7 percent *before inflation*. Taking a macro view of the last seventy-two years as an example, the annual rate of inflation in this country, as measured by growth in CPI, has averaged around 3.1 percent. That means T-bills have actually earned savers a little over 0.5 percent in *real* (inflation-adjusted) interest during that period of time (see Table 7.2).

Table 7.2

Treasury Bills

72-Year (1925–1997) Real Return Average

T-bill interest rate (before inflation)	= 3.7%/yr.
CPI (inflation rate)	= 3.1%/yr.
Total *real* return	**= +0.6%/yr.**

However safe, smooth, and consistently reliable (albeit small) this rate of return looks in the macro view, a close-up, or micro, view of that same period reveals some interesting figures. There have been long periods within that seventy-two-year stretch of time when T-bills provided savers with *negative* real, inflation-adjusted returns, or actual losses on paper of their principal.

For example, from the end of 1932 to the end of 1980, T-bills paid an average of 2.8 percent a year before inflation. But inflation during that almost fifty-year span averaged around 4 percent. So, if you had bought and rolled over your T-bills consistently during those years, you would have averaged a negative real return of minus 1.2 percent a year (see Table 7.3). In other words, after inflation you would have been losing 1.2 percent of your money a year in these supersafe securities. In fact, your loss would have been greater because you would have had to pay taxes each year on the 2.8 percent you were earning even though, in real terms, you were actually losing money.

On the other hand, from the end of 1925 to the end of the 1929–1932 Great Crash, when T-bills were paying a nominal return of 2.7 percent a year, roughly similar to that of the 1932–1980 period (2.8 percent), the country was experiencing 4.4 percent a year *deflation*. As a result, the real return on T-bills during that period of time was 7.1 percent (see Table 7.4).

This may not seem like much to today's bull marketeers, but if,

---

Table 7.3

Treasury Bills

48-Year (1932–1980) Real Return Average

T-bill interest rate (before inflation)	= 2.8%/yr.
CPI (inflation rate)	= 4.0%/yr.
Total *real* return	= –1.2%/yr.

Table 7.4

Treasury Bills

7-Year (1925–1932) Real Return Average

T-bill interest rate (before deflation)	= 2.7%/yr.
CPI (deflation rate)	= 4.4%/yr.
Total *real* return	**= +7.1%/yr.**

for example, you were to look at the performance of small company and blue chip or other large company stocks during that same period, they were producing minus 18.2 percent and minus 3.3 percent negative returns per year, respectively. So, that 2.7 percent a year earnings in nominal terms and 7.1 a year earnings in real returns given off by T-bills—versus *losing* money in the stock market—would have felt pretty good indeed.

More recently, since 1980, T-bill interest rates have been very high—around 6.9 percent, a figure more than double the historical norm of 3.7 percent a year. When the 3.8 percent a year that inflation has been averaging since 1980 is subtracted from that figure, the result shows that T-bill savers have been receiving an average return of 3.1 percent a year in real terms for the past seventeen years (see Table 7.5), or *five times* the normal rate of return T-bills have averaged over the last seventy-two years. That's not a bad reward at all for the comparatively little risk they've assumed to get it.

Table 7.5

Treasury Bills

17-Year (1980–1997) Real Return Average

T-bill interest rate (before inflation)	= 6.9%/yr.
CPI (inflation rate)	= 3.8%/yr.
Total *real* return	**= +3.1%/yr.**

Looking Ahead

Generally speaking, if the outlook for inflation is higher, bond prices will eventually fall and investors are better off in the safe haven of T-bills. But if the outlook is for little or no inflation, interest rates will fall and bond prices will rise. Then investors are better off in longer-term bonds.

The outlook today both in the United States and globally is for weak economies, fierce price competition, and depressed stock prices. That translates into a forecast of low inflation and falling interest rates.

The current yield on a 30-year T-bond is about 6 percent. I think a decline in the near future to 5 percent is almost certain, and that a decline to at least 4 percent is highly likely by the year 2000. Beyond that, if my expectation of actual deflation proves correct, we could get down to around 2 percent early in the next century, just as we did during the deflation era of the 1930s. On that basis, my belief is that investors are better off today, and for the foreseeable future, in T-bonds rather than either T-bills or stocks.

Points to Remember

* If your primary concern is the safe guardianship of your investment dollar, there is no more reliable security than the short-term U.S. Treasury bill, the most liquid investment in the world. However, it is possible to get caught in a long period of time when, for whatever reason, interest rates go up and T-bills fail to keep even with inflation. (The reason typically is people's misperceptions about the outlook for inflation combined with the U.S. government's misguided bias toward inflationary policies, as occurred between 1932 and 1950.) In such a case, negative real returns, after taxes, can be substantial. Therefore, it *is* possible to lose money, especially in

inflation-adjusted terms, even in those ultimate of ultimate safe havens called T-bills.

- It is vital for every investor, experienced or inexperienced, to recognize the fact that there are certain times within market cycles when there are *no* attractive places to make money. The best one can hope for is to hang on to what one has, like those bank-fearing folks of the 1930s. Under such circumstances, T-bills are an ideal depository because one doesn't put money in them expecting to see a high return on one's principal. The objective is the safe return of one's principal until market conditions improve. Everything else is gravy.

- When market conditions and the economy are good, and valuation levels are not off the charts, it is far more preferable to be in other types of investments that are riskier, but will also provide a higher reward for the degree of risk you're taking.

- The key is to know when it's in your interest to take risk, and when discretion is the better part of valor. Sometimes there aren't any profitable opportunities for investment, and the wisest course is to just sit on the sidelines for a while in low-risk, nominally returning T-bills.

- Especially in bear markets, which, as we've seen, have come along quite frequently over the past seventy-two years, T-bills can be the perfect place to hibernate, and get paid relatively handsomely while catching your Zs.

EIGHT

You Should Get Paid for Taking Risk

As a seasoned investor who has personally weathered many major up and down market storms, individual investment cycles, and manias, and studied many more, I have come to believe very strongly that *every investor should be paid for taking risk*.

The financial markets usually agree. That's why in the bond market, buyers almost always receive more interest from lower-rated corporate and junk bonds than from higher-grade bonds issued by AAA-rated companies and the U.S. government.

For example, in today's market, a 30-year U.S. Treasury bond, which has no speculative element, would yield around 4.7 percent while a bond with a speculative element such as a CCC-rated Indonesian, Russian, Brazilian, or Argentine government bond could throw off anywhere from 20 to 60 percent as much as twelve times the return. The degree of risk one assumes buying one bond over another is the main reason for the big difference in yield.

When Moody's and Standard & Poor's, the two major bond rating services, issue their ratings (see Chapter 2), they try to assess two things: first, what is the guarantee the bondholder will be given back his or her principal at maturity; and second, what is the probability the bond issuer will be able to pay the agreed-upon rate of interest from the time of purchase to maturity?

These ratings enable the investor to decide whether or not the potential reward will justify the potential risk. How would stocks fare if the same criteria were applied to today's market? Consider the following questions and answers:

Question: What is the guarantee a stock-issuing company will give shareholders their money back at any point in the future?

Answer: Virtually nil.

Question: What obligation does the same company have to pay investors any dividends or interest while expectant shareholders are waiting to not get their money back?

Answer: None.

Question: If bond rating criteria were applied to stocks, where should stocks trade in relation to bonds?

Answer: Below BB-rated bonds; i.e., the DJIA earnings yield should be above 12 percent, or a P/E of 8.3—which would put the Dow at around 3232, 64 percent below its current price!

Question: Where do they trade?

Answer: *Above* U.S. government bonds (4.3 percent earnings yield versus 5.8 percent for long-term Governments).

What this demonstrates is that in today's overpriced stock market, investors are *not* being sufficiently paid for the risk they're assuming with common stock ownership.

With stocks selling today at an average P/E of 23, the yield on stocks is far lower than the yield on bonds, not higher, as it has been historically. Therefore, today's stock market fiends are *paying the market* for the risk they're taking, not the other way around. To me this concept is not only absurd, but anathema, and should be unacceptable to any prudent investor.

Risk Premium Versus Premium Risk

Risk premium—the amount of extra yield, or extra return, the markets pay investors for taking risks—varies enormously over time.

As an example, in 1950, long-term T-bonds were paying 2.5 percent. DJIA stocks at that time were selling at approximately 6 times earnings, which translates to an intrinsic return of about 16.7 percent. So, without any growth and assuming these companies' earnings stayed exactly the same, this meant investors were getting a 14.2 percent greater return for the risk they were taking with these blue chips than they would have gotten from the less risky T-bonds. In other words, they were being paid roughly 6.7 times as much for the premium risk they were assuming owning those stocks.

Today, the situation is reversed.

Stocks, as I've written, are selling at an average of around 25 times earnings, which translates to an earnings yield, or intrinsic return, of slightly more than 4 percent. Meanwhile, long-term Treasuries are throwing off a return of around 5 percent—that's almost 25 percent more return with a fraction of the risk.

Today's situation is the exception, not the rule.

Historically, investors have been paid substantial risk premiums to invest in stocks. The year 1950 was an extreme case, but generally, the earnings yield on stocks, which, as you'll recall from Chapter 2, is determined by dividing earnings per share by the price of the stock, has almost always been higher than that of quality long-term bonds. This is because, as already noted, stocks have traditionally been known to be riskier than bonds for most of financial history. But there have been times, most of them recent, when the normal relationship between stocks and bonds has experienced a turnaround. One of them is today.

This turnaround typically follows an extended period of high inflation when, even long after inflation has subsided, expectations of its imminent, soaring reappearance—whether well founded or just plain paranoid—continue to haunt the public consciousness like a corpse that won't stay dead. This foments disenchantment with the bond market because investors know that bonds, unlike stocks, cannot be adjusted to keep pace with, let alone stay ahead of, any upward surges in the rate of inflation.

Locked into a fixed semiannual coupon and the return of a fixed sum of current, unprotected dollars at some point in the future, bondholders realize that if inflation shoots up after they buy bonds, they're stuck—as if having caught a bad cold that refuses to go away. But companies can raise the price of their products and make other necessary adjustments to ward off the effects of inflation so that their stocks survive and prosper.

Beginning in 1968, a period of high and rising inflation that reached double digits by 1974, stocks began to trade richer than bonds for all the aforementioned reasons, and the earnings yield on stocks dropped below the earnings yield on long-term Treasuries and AAA-rated corporate bonds for the first time in this century. That condition persisted until the 1973–1974 bear market, when the price of stocks tumbled to a level where they were once again selling cheap relative to bonds, the historical norm.

The price of stocks stayed that way until the end of 1980—a period of sixteen years during which stock and bond valuations fell back to their traditional relationship in terms of risk premium, whereby the earnings yield on stocks was higher than that of bonds.

However, in 1980, interest rates soared as inflation rose into the stratosphere, and investor psychology kicked in, reversing that traditional relationship once more.

Ever since the 1930s, and especially in the 1970s and early 1980s, investors had seen inflation follow a sawtooth pattern of higher highs and higher lows. Even when, cyclically, the Federal Reserve Board would intervene and impose austerity controls to put the brakes on the economy by tightening the money supply and raising short-term interest rates, inflation had never fallen below the low of the previous cycle. So, when inflation reached high double digits in the early 1980s, investors became *convinced* that inflation not only was here to stay but would always rise to new highs, as it had been doing for the past fifty years.

As mentioned in Chapter 6, it wasn't until Ronald Reagan and Federal Reserve Board Chairman Paul Volcker teamed up to put inflation in check—for the foreseeable future, anyway—that this sawtooth pattern really changed. Nevertheless, investors, being creatures of habit prone to fighting the last war and basing their investment choices on past performance, started demanding higher rates of interest for bonds than were justified by the falling rate of inflation.

Consequently, whereas from 1965 to 1980 investors in long-term bonds had received an average of 0.5 percent per year in real terms, bond investors since 1980 have been averaging *more than 5 percent* in real terms.

As I write this, inflation over the last twelve months has been running about 1.7 percent, and appears to be heading farther south still. The Consumer Price Index has seen no upward surge since the late 1980s. Yet, in spite of this currently positive picture of inflationary trends, and no reasonable expectations that trends will change for the worse—actually, I believe that deflation is more likely—long-term Treasury bonds are now paying close to 5 percent (approximately 3.4 percent real interest)—almost the bond market has normally returned throughout history. And T-bills are paying around 5 percent today (about 3.4 percent real interest), more than five times the historical norm of a 0.6 percent *real* return. Mighty attractive indeed!

Stocks meanwhile are giving off real returns of 4 percent, less than half of their historical average. (The same is true of lower-grade bonds.) However, because interest rates have been falling for such a long period of time due to little or no inflation, most investors do not realize that the returns of long-term Treasuries, high-grade corporate bonds, and T-bills are actually way above nor-mal these days. As a result, they're doing what we in the investment business call "reaching for yield" by dropping down in quality.

Generally speaking, the spreads in today's market between low risk (i.e., U.S. T-bonds and T-bills) and high risk (i.e., stocks and junk bonds) are so tight—or inverted, as between stocks and bonds—that the real opportunities for being well compensated to take risk, certainly with stocks, exist mainly in the Asian markets. Stock prices there have fallen so low—almost 80 percent below where they were just a year ago—that they've become bargains. Thus, there is greater potential for higher reward if you're willing to take the risk.

But in the Western markets, particularly those of the United States, Europe, and Japan, dividend yields on stocks, which have historically averaged around 5 percent, are now down below 2 per-cent; and book value, which has traditionally ranged between one and two times book, is now close to five times book! So, outside of the Asian markets, and a few others like Ghana and Venezuela, there's not a lot of risk premium going into stock investors' pockets to compensate for the sizable risk they're taking.

I've provided only a few examples, but they're enough to illus-trate just how expensive stocks have become in relation to their historical levels and patterns of behavior, reinforcing my belief that today's investors are not being paid sufficiently to assume the risk of stock ownership. At the same time, today's investors in bonds, which also entail some risk but not as much as stocks, are being paid substantially higher than normal returns for that risk.

I'm reminded of that old joke by the late Henny Youngman about the guy who feels a sharp a pain in his arm whenever he lifts it. He goes to the doctor for advice, and says, "Doc, it hurts when I do this." The Doc replies, "Then don't do that." O'Higgins' Law about the relationship between risk and reward is: If you're not being rewarded to take risk, *don't take it*! Pure and simple.

Regression to the Mean

If the reader were to review the range of benchmarks measuring the relative valuation of stocks as far back as the 1920s, as I've done for this book, he or she would see that in order to regress to their historic median level, stocks today would have to go down 40 to 50 percent.

By contrast, high-grade bond yields, such as those on long-term U.S. Treasuries, are just below their historic median level of 5 percent (the average inflation rate of 3 percent plus 2 percent real interest), meaning that, if such a regression were to occur, and you bought long-term zero coupon Treasury bonds at their current yield of almost 5 percent, you would earn a respectable total return on your investment, with little risk.

On the other hand, if you bought stocks, you would lose a great deal of money.

The Pit and the Pendulum

Approximately 85 percent of a stock's price is determined by two factors that work hand in glove: investor psychology and economic conditions.

Corporate conditions do not change anywhere near as much as do investor perceptions of those conditions. That is why, at certain times in our history, stocks have sold at 6 times earnings—an earnings yield of close to 17 percent—and at other times, like today, they've sold at 23 times earnings, an earnings yield of a little over 4 percent.

In other words, there are times when, because of psychology and economic conditions, investors are willing to pay only $6 for $1 of earnings, and other times when they're willing to pay $23 for that same $1 of earnings. Same stock-issuing companies, same stocks, same economy, same country, but vastly different perceptions governing the investment decision-making process.

Why does this happen?

Because when investor perceptions undergo a shift, the pendulum starts swinging in a given direction, and a self-reinforcing cycle begins.

In a downward cycle, stocks go down, and keep going down, because as more people lose more money in them, more people become less interested in stocks as an investment. They sell, which forces stock prices further down still, which makes more people sell off, until stocks reach an extreme point where they are selling so cheap that prices can't go down any further and value-conscious investors like myself start picking up the bargains.

When the pendulum swings the other way and an upcycle occurs, the process is merely reversed.

Risk Expansion and Contraction

Regardless of which way the pendulum is swinging, investor risk does not stay constant. It expands and contracts with price, but in reverse ratio to what many investors believe. The irony is that investors tend to apply this ratio correctly to almost every other type of purchase they make, by shopping around for the best buy that will ensure them the least amount of loss if the purchase fails to deliver on its promised reward.

When stocks are selling at 6 times earnings (historically the lowest average P/E at which American stocks have sold), they're *very safe* because there isn't a whole lot more room left for them to go down anymore, but there is a great deal of room for them to go up. In addition, because companies normally pay out around half of their earnings in the form of quarterly dividends, investors are getting paid handsomely while waiting for their stocks to go up.

On the other hand, when stocks reach above-normal price levels—P/Es of 23 to 28 times earnings, like today—the risk of ownership is so much greater because there's a great deal of room for them to go down, but almost no potential room for them to go up.

Even the safest investments can become risky if they get expensive enough.

This was the case with Treasury bonds back in the 1940s, when they were paying 2 percent, and inflation, over time, was averaging 3 percent. It doesn't require a calculator to figure out that if you're getting only 2 percent, and inflation in the long run is 3 percent, you're probably going to be losing 1 percent a year.

However, in 1981, when everyone was getting back into stocks and sowing the seeds for the big bull market stampede we're still in the midst of today, T-bonds were paying 15 percent. Anyone well versed in financial history, and knowing that inflation over time averaged 3 percent, would have recognized that U.S. government-guaranteed 12 percent real, inflation-adjusted interest on a super-safe investment like T-bonds was an unbelievably attractive return.

But investors then, as now, favored stocks over bonds because of their mistaken belief that inflation was forever and that stocks would hold their own while bonds would remain the "certificates of confiscation" that they had been since 1940. Equity investors have certainly done well since 1980, but they would have done even better, with less risk, if they had recognized the compelling values offered by bonds—long-term zero coupon bonds, in particular.

Head Games

The probable explanation for this line of reasoning among investors is that by the time stocks are finally selling cheap again (at, say, 6 times earnings), they've been going down in value a good ten to fifteen years to reach that level. If it takes thirty days to make or break a habit, it's easy to see how a ten- to fifteen-year out-of-favor stock slump could affirm the perception that stocks are unsafe at any price.

For example, by the time stocks returned to 6 times earnings in

1974, they had been steadily going down in value for thirteen years, since 1961. So, anybody who bought stocks during that time lost money. This had such a cumulative effect on investor psychology that by 1974, when stocks were bargains again, offering huge opportunities for reward, investors had become conditioned to view them as toxic waste—*at the precise moment when stocks were least toxic.*

Today, it's as if we're looking through the other side of a two-way mirror. Stocks are very popular now because they've been steadily going up for sixteen-plus years, not having experienced even a 10 percent decline since 1990. So, investors today view stocks as sure bets at the very time when stocks are most vulnerable to a decline, and the least sure bet to provide ample returns for the degree of risk investors are taking by owning them. In fact, investor euphoria is so extreme today that when someone like me suggests the possibility that this big bull market could suffer even an average 30 percent decline (eight of which have occurred since 1960), I'm considered, at best, a wet blanket, and, at worst, a lunatic. But the odds are that if a decline does occur, it will likely be more than the historical average of 30 percent, because the market today is much more overvalued than ever before in history.

By the same token, although bonds have proven themselves to be sound investments over time, today they're perceived as riskier because the greatest threat to bonds remains that pesky specter called inflation, which is still casting its pall on investors and on the monetary authorities, not just in the United States but around the world as well. They persist in believing, in spite of all the contrary evidence staring them in the face, that inflation continues to be a major threat.

But inflation is heading downward to such an extent that, in my opinion, the greater market risk today is deflation, which we're already seeing glimpses of, not only in the Far East, but here as well.

Deflation is a risk to the economy, but as I've said, not a risk to bonds, provided investors hold Treasuries. If you own corporate bonds, deflation's a more risky proposition because corporations can default on their debt obligations if profits head south. But government bonds are immune to deflation risk because the possibility of the U.S. Treasury's defaulting on its debt interest obligations is virtually zero.

Nevertheless, though inflation today is about as low as it's ever been, and projected to either stay that way or go lower still, there remains a strong disconnect between what investors see with their own eyes and what they allow themselves to feel in their hearts and minds.

If one had polled investors a year ago about the most attractive markets in the world, the number one response would probably have been the Orient because it was the fastest-growing, most dynamic market on the planet. Today, just eighteen months later, the Asian markets are in economic disarray. Stock prices have slalomed to record lows.

So, if you polled the same investors who were so excited about the Asian markets a year and a half ago about whether they would invest there now, they'd look at you with a horror-struck expression, and say, "Are you off of your nut?" They wouldn't touch the Asian markets now with a ten-foot pole or a ten-dollar bill.

Yet stocks in those markets now are very cheap, risk premiums are very high, and the economies are stabilizing. So the chances of being well compensated for taking a risk with Asian stocks are better today than when stock prices there were high. And in reality, that risk is probably quite minimal because stock prices there are so far in the basement that they have absolutely nowhere else to go but up, whereas here in the United States and Europe, the risk of losing money in stocks is much higher because stock prices have reached the outer limits. But investors prefer to believe the opposite as they continue playing head games with themselves.

Judgment Call

It's important for investors to be aware of how different investments have been valued over time, what median returns have been, what these different investment vehicles are yielding now, and how to be sufficiently well compensated for the risk of loss by having a return that is assessable in advance.

No one knows for sure, of course, exactly what the future has in store for us. No one knows what the inflation rate's really going to be next year, or the next. No one knows what corporate profits are going to be. But it *is* possible to look at current market conditions, and by comparing our three investment choices to each other in light of those conditions, make a calculated judgment as to which vehicle presents the greatest opportunity for achieving the highest risk-adjusted returns for the degree of risk one is willing to assume.

So, now that you are convinced (I hope) that you should be paid for taking risk, the time has come to assess and quantify the amount you should be getting paid for that risk, and find out how to make the call that will lead you to being rewarded with above-average returns.

PART 3

Knowing Where to Invest

NINE

Basic Risk-Based Asset Allocation

NUMEROUS FINANCIAL STUDIES conclude that proper asset allocation—the process of deciding the percentage of a portfolio to be
invested in each major investment sector (stocks, bonds, and riskless
cash equivalents)—accounts for more than 85 percent of investment
returns. Specific investment selection (buying one particular stock
or bond over another) accounts for less than 15 percent.

Because asset allocation is so widely believed to be the name of
the game, the investment industry spends a lot of time and effort
formulating the ideal mix.

Regrettably, the vast majority of professional investors with
their differing ratios have failed even to match the performance of
the S&P 500. In other words, very few of them are beating the
Dow.

Do You Want to Be an Owner or a Lender?

Asset allocation involves making choices. And the first choice you
must make is whether you want to be an owner or a lender.

As discussed in the previous chapters, there are times when it pays best to be an owner because stocks are selling cheaper than bonds, and other times, which can last quite a number of years, when it's more advantageous to be a lender because the opposite is true.

During most of our history, it has been more profitable to be an owner by buying stocks than to be a lender by buying bonds, because stocks have traditionally sold less expensively than bonds, and have therefore offered more potential for greater reward. But ever since the early 1980s, when the current big bull market began, it's actually been more advantageous for investors to have favored the bond market. Why? Because during this long stampede, stock prices have steadily gone upward and dividend yields have steadily shrunk, rendering cheaper-selling bonds the better buy for your money.

If market prices indicate that being a lender is the way to go, you're now faced with a second, equally important, decision to make. Do you want to be a long-term lender or a short-term lender?

The advantage to lending on a long-term basis is that it locks you into a fixed rate of interest until the bond matures. This means that if interest rates drop during the period until the bond matures, you keep receiving the old, high rate of interest, which you can either spend or reinvest. Not only that, because newly issued bonds would then be paying a lower rate of interest, the value of your long-term bonds increases, and you can be rewarded quite handsomely.

But as described in Chapter 6, there also are significant risks involved in lending long-term, particularly in the corporate and municipal bond market; these risks could result in the loss of your principal. Thus, the advantage to lending on a short-term basis, even if buying corporate and municipal bonds, is that there is much less risk of losing your principal because there is much less time during which you're at risk. In addition, should interest rates spike upward, you have the opportunity to reinvest your money at those higher rates down the road. But if you've invested long-term, you're stuck with the interest rate you locked into when you initially loaned the money.

Practice Makes (Almost) Perfect

Although asset allocation is a valuable—indeed *essential*—investment tool, it is all too often avoided by large numbers of investors, as well as by some people in my own business of asset management. There are several reasons why this is so.

One is that they just don't know *how* to do it. And, of course, the natural human inclination when one doesn't know how to do something is to avoid doing it.

The other reason is that when the market moves in only one direction for an extended period of time, it's a lot easier just to join in and go with the flow; in fact, going with the flow becomes virtually an ingrained attitude. This is why the majority of today's so-called professional money managers, investment advisors, and market pundits, having lived through a stock market that, for the most part, has been steadily going up over the past several decades, say, "Why give yourself a headache trying to decide whether to allocate your assets? The easiest and most profitable way to participate is to keep buying and holding common stocks and just forget about other alternatives."

Typically, this attitude reaches its zenith at the end of a long stock market upcycle, where I believe we are now, a period when the whole idea of asset allocation, or "timing the market" as it is also called, is held in particularly low regard. The assumption is that since stocks have continually gone up, they'll keep going up.

The prevailing attitude toward asset allocation is exactly the reverse at the end of a long downmarket cycle. For example, when today's big bull stampede began its initial sprint at the end of the 1973–1974 bear market, the greatest heroes on Wall Street were the "market timers" who, having accurately predicted the bear's demise, recommended a buy-and-sell stocks strategy. Today, the greatest heroes on Wall Street are the Warren Buffetts of the world who buy, hold, and never sell.

The idea that, because asset allocation isn't an exact science, it is very difficult to do, is not without some merit, however. Many factors influence the price of securities, and thus determine the advantages of investing in one type of security over another (and when). Establishing a preference can seem both perplexing and daunting.

I'm with you. The more abstract, complex, or labor-intensive a process is, the more it begins to border on migraine-producing quantum mechanics, the less inclined I am to avail myself of it. In fact, I'm more prone to throw up my hands and head in the opposite direction.

But I believe difficult doesn't have to mean impossible; that everything—except perhaps the workings of the universe (and maybe even those too, someday)—can be boiled down into some straightforward, user-friendly nuts and bolts that are understandable to everyone.

My investment philosophy has always been to *keep it simple*. And so I have come up with some relatively simple, practice-makes-perfect (or as close to perfect as one can get in the investment biz) ways that remove some of the mystery from the asset allocation process, and make it easier to determine your investment preferences year after year. I call them my "Seventeen Steps to Super Returns," and I'll roll them out in full in the next chapter. But for now I want to stick with the broad-brush concept of asset allocation, which is *so* important, by playing a little game with you to which I've given the somewhat oxymoronic title of "Looking Forward with Hindsight."

Take a peek at Figure 9.1, which we first encountered in Chapter 4. It shows the year-by-year performance of each major investment sector—large company stocks, small company stocks, long-term corporate bonds, long-term U.S. Government Treasury bonds, and U.S Treasury bills—from 1925 to 1997.

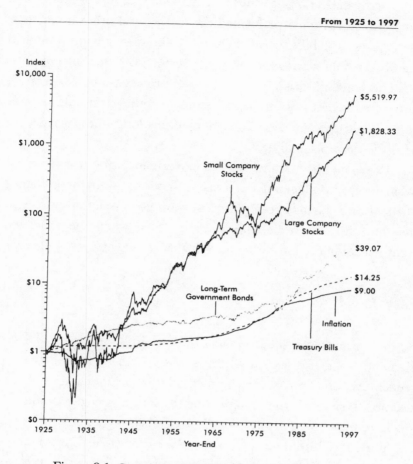

Figure 9.1. Cumulative Wealth Indices of Common Stocks,
Government, Corporate, and Municipal Bonds, and T-Bills, 1925–1997.

This seventy-plus-year snapshot graphically illustrates the
value of asset allocation. Given the fact—which we seem to have
forgotten these days, but which Figure 9.1 serves to potently
remind us—that no single investment vehicle performs best all the
time, we can now see the results we would have achieved year after
year from having known in advance which sector was the place to
be for the choicest returns in the coming year.

As seen, small company stocks have clearly been the best-
performing sector during the last seventy-odd years. But there were

many individual years, as well as many longer periods of time, when small cap stocks underperformed the market and other investment sectors—even T-bills, which Figure 9.1 shows as having produced the worst results among the five major sectors over that span of time.

The conclusion is obvious. There were occasions when small caps were the best place to be, occasions when they were the second-best place to be, and occasions, sometimes long ones, when they were the *worst* place to be.

If we could have improved the performance of our investment in small caps by allocating our assets—that is to say, by stepping out of small caps during those off years, profitably going elsewhere in the meantime, then stepping back in again when the time was right—wouldn't that have been a valuable strategy to have pursued?

Easy Does It

As I've written, asset allocation involves making a series of bold decisions up front, the first of which is whether to be an owner or a lender. I've found a very efficient method for making that critical first decision. It simply involves comparing the earnings yield on common stocks to the yield to maturity on AAA-rated corporate bonds.

You'll recall from Chapter 4 that the earnings yield on common stocks is easily computed by taking the current average price to earnings ratio and turning it around to arrive at a figure expressed as a percentage. For example, if stocks are currently selling at 28 times earnings, turn that around and you get an earnings yield of 3.6 percent.

The yield to maturity on AAA-rated corporate bonds is arrived at by looking up the current rate of interest on 10-year U.S. Government bonds and adding 0.3 percent (or 30 basis points) to that figure. For example, as I write this, the interest rate on 10-year T-bonds is 4.3 percent. Add 0.3 percent to that and you get 4.6 percent.

Now compare the two different yields. As common stocks are selling expensively today at 28 times earnings, an earnings yield of 3.6 percent, and AAA-rated corporate bonds are yielding an estimated 5.8 percent, the earnings yield on common stocks is *below* that of AAA-rated bonds. Thus, as AAA-rated bonds are selling cheaper than stocks, and are the better buy in terms of potentially greater reward, it pays more to be a lender in today's market than an owner. There's your decision.

If you look at Figure 9.2, which tracks the earnings yield on the S&P 500 relative to that of bonds rated AAA by Moody's from the 1940s to the present, you'll see that from the mid-1940s to the late 1960s, when stocks sold cheaper than bonds, the earnings yield on the former was almost always well above that on the latter.

The reason is simple. Investors, or the market in general, had decided that because stocks were inherently riskier than bonds, they had to be paid a substantial premium in terms of initial return, measurable by the earnings, to justify the risk of investing in stocks. In other words, without making any predictions as to what earnings in the future might be, they looked at stocks versus bonds in terms of current profitability, and said, "Okay, the total earnings as a percentage of the price on stocks is 10 percent; bond yields are 3 percent. Stocks are selling cheaper than bonds because 10 percent beats 3 percent, so stocks are the place to be."

However, from 1968 until 1974, the earnings yield on stocks dropped below that of bonds as stocks became more expensive than bonds; therefore, in terms of risk premium versus premium risk, they were less attractive than bonds during that six-year period.

Then, during the 1973–1974 bear market, the price of stocks went down precipitously, to a point where, from the end of 1974 to the end of 1980, stocks were consistently selling cheaper than bonds. And guess what happened? Stocks, in general, dramatically outperformed bonds during that time period, whereas in the earlier six-year period from 1968 to 1974, when bonds were cheaper than stocks, bonds outperformed stocks.

Another valuation shift occurred at the end of 1980, when stocks began selling more expensively than bonds, a pattern that has continued right up to the present moment. Because this latest period in which bonds have consistently sold cheaper than stocks hasn't ended and another valuation shift occurred, the final results of overall market performance between stocks and bonds are not in yet. But given the fact that bonds have sold cheaper than stocks for the last eighteen years, and that our Figure 9.1 record of past results shows that buying cheaper means greater earnings potential, this would seem to indicate that, since 1980, being a lender rather than an owner has been the way to go.

However, if we compare the yield on stocks to the yield on short-term, regular coupon bonds during this same span of time, the stock market has consistently outperformed the bond market.

"Hold on a minute!" you might suddenly shout in confusion, rubbing your brow as you ponder the investment wisdom bestowed upon you. "If that's the case and I *had* followed your advice and gone into bonds in 1980, I wouldn't have made as much as I would have in stocks!"

"Hold on, yourself!" I reply. "Choosing to be a lender rather than an owner is not enough. Don't forget decision number two in the asset allocation scheme of things. What kind of lender in the bond market is it that you choose to be? Long-term? Or short?"

If you had put your money in a type of security that first began to appear in the late 1970s and early 1980s called the 30-year zero coupon U.S Government Treasury bond, you would have earned *more money* in the last eighteen years buying and holding that investment than you would have earned in the S&P 500—a result that not even 90 percent of professional money managers came close to matching during that period of time! And you would have achieved that result virtually without having to do any work, paying any fees, or losing any sleep at night worrying about the 1981–1982 bear market, the crash of 1987—none of that.

The bottom line: As important as the decision of whether to be a lender in the bond market or an owner in the stock market is, the choice of where you're going to allocate your assets in the bond market, assuming that's your direction, is just as important.

So, the question now becomes: How do I make that second critical decision?

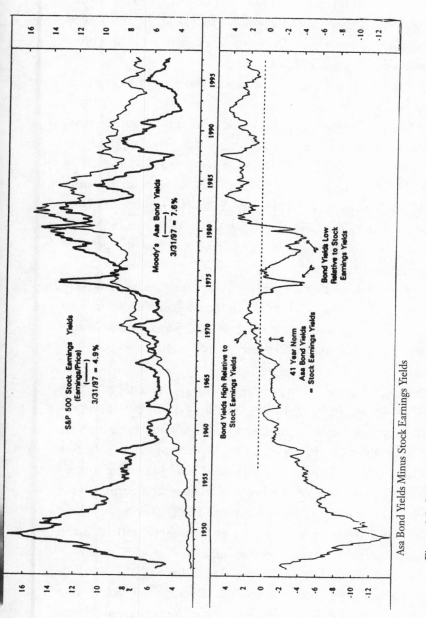

Asa Bond Yields Minus Stock Earnings Yields

Figure 9.2. S&P 500 Stock Earnings Yield versus Moody's AAA-Rated Bond Yield, 1940–1994.

Source: Ned Davis Research.

O'Higgins's Bond Market Indicator

As demonstrated in Chapter 6, bonds can be risky, too. Not only can they go down, they can go down a great deal. So, it's just as critical to protect your capital by avoiding downturns in the bond market as it is in the stock market.

And I've found a very easy way of doing this too. Just keep your eye on the *price of gold*.

It has been true historically that when inflation or other anxieties have dominated market psychology, the price of gold has risen. This was dramatically illustrated in January 1980, when high international inflation, led by rising oil prices, tension surrounding the American hostage crisis in the late Ayatollah Khomeini's Iran, and civil unrest in oil-rich Saudi Arabia, drove the price of gold to $887.50 per ounce before calmer times returned and the price of gold stabilized at lower levels.

The price of gold first began to trade freely in the marketplace at the end of 1968. So it's really been available to us as a potential indicator of upcoming market conditions for just thirty years now. But in terms of reliability, it has definitely stood the test of time.

As shown in Figure 9.1 at the beginning of this chapter, from 1968 to 1997 investors lost money in the long-term U.S. Government Treasury bond market nine out of those twenty-nine years. But if they'd relied on the change in the price of gold from one year to the next as an indicator, they would have been able to correctly predict the course of the bond market in the coming year *twenty-eight out of those twenty-nine years*. Thus, they would have known in advance that it was time to go elsewhere, either in the fixed-income security market, or perhaps into stocks, and they would have avoided each of those nine downturns.

Conversely, if they were invested elsewhere, they would have known by relying on the same indicator that the bond market was on the verge of an upswing in the coming year, and would have been able to act profitably on that knowledge in advance also.

As Figure 9.1 shows, just by having allocated your assets—or zigzagging—between the two different fixed-income sectors (riskless 1-year Treasury bills and the opposite extreme, long-term U.S. Government Treasury bonds) and not even venturing into the third sector, the scary world of the stock market, you would have averaged returns during that time of more than 20 percent a year (before transaction costs)—with only one down year, in 1977. Compare those results with what would have been achieved if you hadn't zigzagged but just bought long-term U.S. Government Treasury bonds every year and stayed with them during that period, earning 8.7 percent a year and experiencing nine down years. Zigzagging was a mighty more rewarding strategy, don't you agree?

Not Foolproof

However, the price of gold is not a completely foolproof indicator—because twenty-eight out of twenty-nine times is not a perfect score.

But believe me, in the investment business (or *any* business, for that matter), hitting the bull's-eye twenty-eight out of twenty-nine times—which equates to 97 percent accuracy—is not only pretty darn good, it is almost unique.

Comparing Results

As seen in Table 9.1, my new Beating the Dow system of allocating assets between T-bonds, T-bills, and stocks would have selected stocks as the asset class of choice in only eight of the past twenty-nine years. And it would have indicated staying in riskless T-bills and guaranteed U.S. Government Treasury bonds for an almost equal number of the remaining twenty-one years.

While buy-and-hold investors in the S&P would have lost money in six of the last twenty-nine years, those using my new system would have suffered a loss in just one, with a minus 3.8 percent negative return in 1974.

As described in Chapter 1, my Beating the Dow Five-Stock Strategy is still the stock-picking system to beat when the investment class of choice is determined to be stocks. But for all the reasons stated throughout this book, it no longer responds sufficiently to the overall needs of investors in today's market because it is only one-third of a strategy.

My new strategy of allocating assets among and between the three major investment sectors closes the loop by being more well-rounded. It is the *complete* strategy for winning, not just in today's market conditions but *all* market conditions.

As dramatic proof of how much more effective and profitable a strategy it is, refer to Table 9.2, which shows how often, and by how much, it would have beaten the returns of my Five-Stock Strategy over the past twenty-eight years.

But it is Figure 9.3, perhaps, that tells the tale most vividly. It shows the results my new Beating the Dow Asset Allocation Strategy has produced in cumulative returns versus those of the DJIA and my Beating the Dow Five-Stock Strategy over the past twenty-eight years.

Almost *twenty* times the cumulative return (new system's 47,886 percent versus the DJIA's 2,640 percent) and almost *four times* the cumulative return (new system's 47,886 percent versus Beating the Dow Five-Stock's 12,377 percent)—with *less risk*—may sound like results that are too good to be true. But they aren't.

They are totally in keeping with my contrarian philosophy that buying unpopular and undervalued assets leads to higher, steadier returns over time. They clearly show that asset allocation is not

Table 9.1

Beating the Dow with T-bonds, T-bills, and Stocks
Asset Allocation Strategy Results, 1969–1997

The following table shows the results that my new system for beating the Dow in all market conditions would have produced each year since 1969. It involves deciding once per year whether to invest in T-bonds, T-bills, or stocks (using my Beating the Dow Five-Stock Strategy), then doing nothing for the next twelve months.

Year Ended	Indicated Strategy	CPI 30 yr Inflation	30 yr Zeros	DJIA Return	BTD 5 Stock	O'Higgins New Strategy
12/31/69	1-year T-Bills	6.11%	-17.34%	-11.60%	-10.09%	
12/31/70	30-year Zeros	5.49%	24.33%	8.76%	-4.72%	
12/31/71	1-year T-Bills	3.36%	19.96%	9.79%	5.03%	
12/29/72	1-year T-Bills	3.41%	6.21%	18.21%	22.16%	5.37%
12/31/73	1-year T-Bills	8.80%	-29.59%	-13.12%	19.64%	6.76%
12/31/74	BTD 5 Stock	12.20%	-15.43%	-23.14%	-3.80%	-3.80%
12/31/75	BTD 5 Stock	7.01%	11.34%	44.40%	70.10%	70.10%
12/31/76	BTD 5 Stock	4.81%	32.54%	22.72%	40.80%	40.80%
12/31/77	BTD 5 Stock	6.77%	-10.78%	-12.70%	4.50%	4.50%
12/29/78	BTD 5 Stock	9.03%	-16.35%	2.69%	1.70%	1.70%
12/31/79	BTD 5 Stock	13.31%	-20.52%	10.52%	9.90%	9.90%
12/31/80	BTD 5 Stock	12.40%	-33.67%	21.41%	40.50%	40.50%
12/31/81	1-year T-Bills	8.94%	-28.62%	-3.40%	0.00%	13.25%
12/31/82	30-year Zeros	3.87%	156.12%	25.79%	37.40%	156.12%
12/30/83	1-year T-Bills	3.80%	-20.10%	25.68%	36.10%	10.03%
12/31/84	30-year Zeros	3.95%	20.44%	1.05%	12.60%	20.44%
12/31/85	30-year Zeros	3.77%	106.90%	32.78%	37.80%	106.90%
12/31/86	1-year T-Bills	1.13%	74.45%	26.92%	27.90%	5.92%
12/31/87	1-year T-Bills	4.41%	-25.90%	6.02%	11.10%	5.21%
12/30/88	1-year T-Bills	4.42%	7.51%	15.95%	18.40%	8.99%
12/29/89	30-year Zeros	4.65%	45.25%	31.71%	10.50%	45.25%
12/30/90	30-year Zeros	6.11%	0.33%	-0.58%	-15.20%	0.33%
12/31/91	30-year Zeros	3.06%	35.79%	23.93%	61.90%	35.79%

Table 9.1 (cont.)

12/31/92	30-year Zeros	2.90%	7.82%	7.35%	23.20%	7.82%
12/31/93	30-year Zeros	2.75%	39.47%	16.74%	34.30%	39.47%
12/30/94	1-year T-Bills	2.67%	-26.28%	4.98%	8.60%	7.15%
12/29/95	30-year Zeros	2.54%	85.11%	36.49%	30.50%	85.11%
12/31/96	1-year T-Bills	3.32%	-12.58%	28.61%	26.00%	5.49%
12/31/97	30-year Zeros	1.83%	29.22%	24.74%	20.02%	29.22%
9/30/98	30-year Zeros	1.19%	24.39%	0.46%	6.41%	24.39%
Annual		**5.26%**	**9.02%**	**11.66%**	**18.03%**	**23.77%**

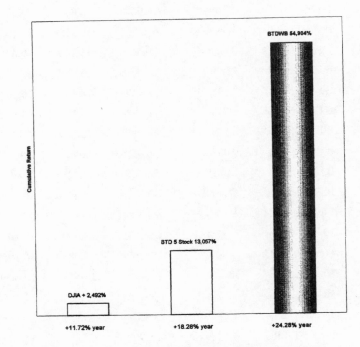

Figure 9.3. Beating the Dow Asset Allocation Beats
Beating the Dow with Bonds, Treasury Bills, and Stocks.
BTD Five-Stock, DJIA Cumulative Returns, and CPI, 12/31/68–12/31/97

Table 9.2

**Beating the Dow Asset Allocation Beats
Beating the Dow Five-Stock**

Number of Years	Period	Returns
4 out of 6 years	12/68–12/74	66.7%
19 out of 28 years	12/68–12/96	67.9%
15 out of 22 years	12/74–12/96	68.2%
10 out of 16 years	12/81–12/97	66.7%

only worth doing—and truly *is* the name of the game—but that it can also be accomplished without a lot of blood, sweat, and tears.

Introduced in the next chapter, my new system will teach you, the average investor, how to decide after less than a half hour of research annually whether to be in stocks, long-term U.S. Government zero coupon Treasury bonds, or 1-year T-bills—and beat the pros again and again by picking the right asset class in order to produce outstanding returns year after year.

Having said that, now it's time to roll up our sleeves and get to work.

TEN

Tying It All Together for Maximum Returns

In INVESTING, as in life, most people tend to complicate decision-making in direct proportion to the importance of the decision being made.

Since money is generally thought to be number one or number two on everyone's list of priorities, most people, when faced with tens of thousands of investment options, become confounded and confused over making investment decisions. They waste an inordinate amount of time and energy which, far too often, produce only unsatisfactory results.

Here's another O'Higgins axiom: Unsatisfactory results prove that the quality of time you put in, not the quantity, is what really pays off in the end. In other words, working smarter beats working harder any day.

One of the most important lessons I have learned from the financial markets is that there is nothing to do 99 percent of the time. Now that you're armed with a knowledge of T-bonds, T-bills, stocks, and my basic risk allocation system, this chapter will show you how to spend that time. By using my Asset Allocation Worksheet and seventeen-step Beating the Dow with T-bonds, T-bills, and Stocks strategy, it will show you when just to sit and watch and when to act.

Unlike anything else on the market, this simple strategy has historically, and with remarkable consistency, outperformed the Dow and the average money manager in creating winning portfolios year after year.

Seventeen Simple Steps to Super Returns

Here are the seventeen easy-to-follow steps to producing remarkable returns in any market condition:

Step 1: Determine Your Investment Fund

Every journey, including the road to greater investment riches, begins with careful preparation, measures you should take that will help you commit yourself to the task ahead and enable you to see it through to the end. As with all journeys, the first thing you should do is make a list of supplies; in this case, that list comes down to a single word: money.

Before you do anything else, you must decide not only how much money you *want* to invest but how much money you *can afford* to invest. Whether it's $5,000 or $100,000, the rule of thumb is simply this: *Don't invest money you are going to need.*

Investing is a gamble, and though my winning formula for Beating the Dow with T-bonds, T-bills, and Stocks does much to eliminate the amount of risk you're taking, there will always be some. My new formula, like any other sound investment strategy, is predicated upon the concept of allowing your money to grow over time, regardless of which asset class is determined to be the optimal choice from one year to the next. This means not having to tap into your investment account because you suddenly find yourself strapped for cash. So, don't use those extra dollars you've got in reserve for living expenses and emergency situations, or that money you've set aside for your child's education or your own retirement, especially if those needs are short-term. The money you use should be earmarked free and clear: "For Investment Purposes Only."

Making the critical determination of how much capital you'll be able to invest without jeopardizing your standard of living itself requires careful preparation, which you can do on your own, or better yet, with the help and guidance of a certified financial planning professional. Whichever route you go, here's what to do:

- Analyze your situation—how much you have in assets, how much debt load you're carrying, how much you're receiving in income, and how much of that income is going toward expenses.
- Establish your major financial goals—buying a home, financing your child's college education, starting a small business, saving for vacations, planning for retirement, or whatever.
- Establish a *realistic* budget plan—a reasonable estimate of your projected income and expenses that covers all your *essential* needs without forcing you to have to scrimp and cut corners. Being unrealistic is the major reason most budget plans fail. Cover all the bases: buying medical and life insurance, putting money in a reserve fund for financial emergencies (most financial planners recommend setting aside three to six months' income in such a fund), saving regularly toward those financial goals you've established, and, perhaps most important of all, the money you'll need to indulge those daily luxuries that make life worth living. As the saying goes, "All work and no play make Jack a dull boy."

Among other things, a financial planner will provide an objective voice in this process, especially when it comes to smoking out your degree of risk tolerance—the amount of risk you're emotionally comfortable and willing to take, and with how much, in the always speculative world of equity investing. Everybody's degree of risk tolerance is different, and it usually changes with time as people age. For example, older investors tend to be more risk-averse than younger investors, just as experienced investors tend to be more prone to taking risks than inexperienced ones—although in today's market, it seems, all such bets are off.

Suffice it to say this: If you break out into a cold sweat whenever you plunk down a dollar for a lottery ticket, then the investing game isn't for you, no matter how good the strategy is, even mine.

Step 2: Open an Investment Account

Once you've decided how much you're going to invest, it's time to select a broker (provided you don't already have one) and open an account so you'll be ready to go as soon as you've completed the remaining steps of my asset allocation formula.

To open an account, you'll be asked to fill out an application form and send the broker a check. Most brokers require a minimum deposit of between $1,000 and $10,000 to open an account with them (the average minimum is around $2,000) plus two to three weeks for the check to clear. Therefore, you should begin this process in advance so that all the processing and paperwork will be done by the time you're ready to make your investment selection.

In Chapter 4, I explained the general differences between, plus the advantages and disadvantages of, the two basic types of brokers—full service and discount—as well as the insurance protection you should look for in selecting a broker. So there's no need to repeat that information here. Just keep in mind when selecting a broker that every dollar you pay in commission and other fees is another dollar you have to earn back on your investment just to come out even. The beauty of this book, as I noted earlier also, is that it does most of the work for you—work that is normally provided, for a hefty fee, by a full-service broker; so, all you really need is a low-cost order taker, the basic service that every discount broker provides.

A third type of broker—the *deep* discount broker—has also entered the scene in recent years due to the emergence of the Internet as a vehicle for faster, equally efficient, and cheaper *online trading*.

A short while back, there were perhaps a couple dozen deep discount brokerage firms offering online trading. Today, that number has tripled, and more firms are getting into it each month. Many small and medium-sized brokerage firms are not online as yet. But most of the biggest ones are, and there's a wide variety of others to choose from; some of whom even trade exclusively online. Many deep discount online brokers provide the same services that traditional discount brokers do, except that their fees for those services are even cheaper.

It's not only faster but—in keeping with my philosophy—*simpler* to execute trades online. Other advantages include the availability of real-time market news and quotes; access twenty-four hours a day, seven days a week; plus, trades can usually be accomplished at a price that traditional trading methods can't match.

To trade online, you must first open an account by filling out an application form as well. But this can be done electronically right on your computer, and forwarded instantaneously with a click of a button without having to resort to the time-consuming U.S. mail. The broker walks you through this and every other stage of the online investing process in easy-to-understand language; all you have to do is be able to read.

Of course, you will also have to deposit a check to open your account, and that *will* require the U.S. mail; the same two to three weeks for the check to clear applies here as well. Or you can transfer the money electronically directly from your bank account, which will cut the time down to about a day. It is a little more complicated, but it's a lot faster, and you can earn interest the entire time that your check would be in the mail or waiting to be credited to your brokerage account. The same requirement of a minimum deposit in the same $1,000 to $10,000 ballpark usually applies also.

Some online brokers may also require you to buy their proprietary software, which will allow you direct access to your account so you can review your portfolio, check the latest market news, and execute trades. But most now offer their proprietary software for free. You can connect to some deep discount brokers via the commercial online services such as America Online, CompuServe, Prodigy Internet, Microsoft Investor, WebTV, and AT&T WorldNet. But if you know how to hop onto the Internet, you can skip to any online broker of your choice and execute trades directly with them.

A lot has been written about the safety of investing online over the Internet due to the Web's susceptibility to invasion of privacy by computer hackers, or "crackers" as they are also called. But recognizing that security is a critical issue to investors—who are already concerned enough about risk—online brokers have made great strides in increasing safeguards against this problem. Today, investing online is as safe as—perhaps even more secure than—placing the average mail order by credit card. Each online broker explains what its safeguards are in an easy-to-access section of its Web page.

Discount and deep discount brokerage commissions and fees range all over the map, and better deals are coming along all the time due to the ever expanding heat of competition. Rates and minimums for equity market orders, limit orders, and brokerage-assisted orders (see Chapter 11 for an explanation of these terms and what's involved) differ from one broker to another, sometimes dramatically.

Some brokers today are charging as little as $5 to $10 for market and limit orders up to 5,000 shares, but the average is usually between $14.95 and $19.95 up to 5,000 shares. Rates typically climb to between $0.01 and $0.03 per 5,000 shares thereafter. Others charge a flat fee of anywhere from $15 to $20 per trade up to 1,000 shares, and require no minimum deposit or minimum balance to open an account. Rates typically go up a few bucks for

Touch-Tone phone ordering via the broker's 800 number. And virtually all discount and deep discount brokers charge additional fees for broker-assisted orders if you feel that the need to speak to someone outweighs the cost of doing so.

You can open an account to buy U.S. Treasury securities commission-free directly from the government via its Treasury Direct program (see Chapter 2), a service that has now been made available online as well. You can buy U.S. Treasury securities through most discount and deep discount brokers also, but here again the commissions and fees they charge are all over the place.

Depending upon the broker, they range today from $5 to $14.95 per bond up to 50 bonds, and $2.50 to $49.95 per bond for 51 up to 100-plus bonds. A minimum fee is usually charged for very small orders; typically it is around $40. Commissions on T-bills range from $25 to $49.95 per transaction.

The following list includes a random selection of the more well-known, low-cost, and user-friendly discount and deep discount brokerages that buy and sell T-bonds, T-bills, and stocks. I've purposely not included the specific commission and fee information pertaining to each of them because, as I said, this information keeps changing all the time and would likely be out of date the minute this book hit the stores. You can get the specifics and find out all the other relevant information about opening an account and trading with these brokers easily enough by contacting them directly. Their mailing addresses, 800 numbers, and Web sites are included so that you can make that contact now and in the future, by whichever method you prefer.

Discount and Deep Discount Brokerage Firms

Ameritrade
P.O. Box 2209
Omaha, NB 68103-2209
800-454-9272
www.ameritrade.com

Brown & Company
One Beacon Street
Boston, MA 02108-3102
800-222-2829
www.brownco.com

Burke, Christensen & Lewis Securities, Inc.
Suite 400
303 West Madison Street
Chicago, IL 60606
800-621-0392
www.bclnet.com

Charles Schwab & Co., Inc.
10 Mongomery Street
San Francisco, CA 94104
800-435-4000
www.schwab.com

CompuTel Securities
One 2nd Street
Floor 5
San Francisco, CA 94105
800-432-0327
www.computel.com

Datek Online
100 Wood Avenue South
Iselin, NJ 08830-2716
888-463-2835
www.datek.com

Discover Brokerage Direct (A division of Morgan Stanley,
   Dean Witter, Discover & Co.)
P.O. Box 7037
San Francisco, CA 94120-7037
800-584-6837
www.discoverbrokerage.com

Donaldson, Lufkin & Jenrette
One Pershing Plaza
Jersey City, NJ 07399
800-825-5873
www.DLJdirect.com

Dreyfus Brokerage Services
401 N. Maple Drive
Beverly Hills, CA 90210
800-416-7113
www.tradepbs.com

Empire Financial Group, Inc.
2170 West State Road 434
Suite 124
Longwood, FL 32779
800-900-8101
www.lowfees.com

E*TRADE Securities, Inc.
2400 Geng Road
Palo Alto, CA 94303
800-786-2575
www.etrade.com

Fidelity Brokerage Services, Inc.
100 Summer Street
Boston, MA 02110
800-544-0118
www.fidelity.com

Freedom Investments, Inc.
11422 Miracle Hills Drive
Suite 501
Omaha, NB 68154
800-944-4033
www.freedominvestments.com

InterTrade Securities, Inc.
One Hallidie Plaza
Suite 405
San Francisco, CA 91402
415-616-5982
www.protrade.com

Investex Securities Group
50 Broad Street
New York, NY 10004
800-392-7192
www.investexpress.com

InvestTrade (A division of Regal Discount Securities, Inc.)
950 North Milwaukee Avenue
Suite 102
Glenview, IL 60025
800-498-7120
www.investrade.com

J.B. Oxford Company
9665 Wilshire Blvd, Third Floor
Beverly Hills, CA 90212
800-500-8820
www.jboxford.com

National Discount Brokers
7 Hanover Street
Fourth Floor
New York, NY 10004
800-888-3999
www.ndb.com

Jack White & Company
9191 Towne Center Drive
Second Floor
San Diego, CA 92122
800-431-3500
www.jackwhiteco.com

Quick & Reilly, Inc.
P.O. Box 874
Bowling Green Station
New York, NY 10274-0874
800-837-7220
www.quick-reilly.com

SureTrade, Inc.
P.O. Box 98
Bowling Green Station
New York, NY 10274-0098
800-362-6275
www.suretrade.com

Trade Fast and Preferred Capital Markets, Inc.
220 Montgomery Street
Suite 777
San Francisco, CA 94104
888-781-0283
www.tradefast.com

York Securities, Inc.
160 Broadway
East Building, Tenth Floor
New York, NY 10038
800-362-10038
www.tradingdirect.com

Step 3: Prepare an Asset Allocation Worksheet

Clip out Figure 10.1 and use it as is. Or, if you want to keep your copy of the book intact for future reference (and as a possible collector's item), you can either photocopy it or take a sheet of paper and reproduce Figure 10.1 by dividing the sheet into seven spaces, as shown. Following the same form used in Figure 10.1, label each space as indicated, and add blank lines in the appropriate places so that you will be able to list the data gleaned from your research and make your calculations.

1. S&P Earnings Yield	_____%
2. 10-Year U.S. Gov't T-bond Yield to Maturity	_____%
3.	+ 0.30 %
4. Estimated 10-Year AAA Corporate Bond Yield	_____%
5. [10-Year AAA Corporate Yield]	_____%
[Minus]	–
[S&P Earnings Yield]	_____%
6. Last Week Gold Price Per Troy Ounce	_____
7. Year-Ago Gold Price Per Troy Ounce	_____
8. One-Year Change in Gold Price (Plus or Minus)	_____

Figure 10.1. Beating the Dow with T-bonds, T-bills, and Stocks
Asset Allocation Worksheet.

As this worksheet serves as your portfolio indicator for the entire year, hold on to it; keep it someplace safe where you'll easily be able to find it again (See Figure 10.1)

Step 4: Begin Your Research

On or about January first, buy the latest issue of *Barron's*, the tabloid-sized business and financial newspaper published weekly by Dow Jones & Company; it's available at any large newsstand for $3.

Step 5: Locate P/Es and Yields

Turn to the pullout section titled "Market Week" located in the center of the newspaper and find the index to the week's statistics at the bottom of the page; under the column headed "The Indexes," look up the page number for "P/Es and Yields," then turn to that page.

Step 6: List Latest Standard & Poor's Earnings Yield

Referring to the column of statistics in the top left-hand corner of the page, locate the fifth box in the column dealing with the Standard & Poor's Industrial Index; identify last week's S&P "Earnings Yield %," and list that number in space 1 on your Asset Allocation Worksheet.

Step 7: Locate T-bond Price Quotes

Refer back to the "Market Week" index to the week's statistics; under the column at the bottom of the page headlined "The Markets," locate the page for "Bonds," which contains the latest U.S. Government Treasury bond price quotations, then turn to that section.

Step 8: List Latest Long-Term T-bond Yield

In the box marked "U.S. Notes and Bonds," locate, under the column labeled "Mo/Yr," the most recently issued U.S. Government Treasury bond scheduled to mature in ten years, and list the identified yield to maturity in space 2 of your Asset Allocation Worksheet.

Step 9: Estimate Long-Term AAA Corporate Bond Yield

In space 3 of your Asset Allocation Worksheet, add 0.30 percent (30 basis points) to the 10-year U.S. Government Treasury bond's yield to maturity so that you will arrive at an estimated average yield to maturity for 10-year AAA-rated corporate bonds.

Step 10: Calculate the Difference in Yield

Subtract the S&P earnings yield listed in space 1 of your Asset Allocation Worksheet from your estimated 10-year AAA-rated corporate bond yield average, and list the result in space 4 of your worksheet.

Step 11: Rank the Yields

If the result you came up with in Step 10 *exceeds* the S&P earnings yield, go to Step 12. But if the S&P earnings yield *exceeds* that result, this indicates that stocks are the asset class of choice, in which case proceed directly to Chapter 11 and follow my basic Five-Stock Strategy for beating the Dow.

Step 12: Locate Market Indicators

Go back to the "Market Week" page again; at the bottom of the page under the column marked "The Indicators," locate the page containing the prices of gold and silver, then turn to that section, which bears the general headline "Market Laboratory—Economic Indicators."

Step 13: List Latest Gold Price

Locate the box entitled "Gold & Silver Prices"; under the first boldface heading in the box marked HANDY & HARMAN, note last week's price of gold per troy ounce, which appears in the first column, and list that price in space 5 of your Asset Allocation Worksheet.

Step 14: List Year-Ago Gold Price

Again under HANDY & HARMAN, locate the price of gold per troy ounce of a year ago appearing in the far right column, and list that price in space 6 of your Asset Allocation Worksheet.

Step 15: Compare Gold Prices

Calculate whether the latest price of gold per troy ounce is higher or lower than the year-ago price, then list the one-year change in price, plus or minus, in space 7 of your Asset Allocation Worksheet.

Step 16: Select Your Portfolio and Place Your Order

If the one-year change in the price of gold is on the plus side (*higher* than the price a year ago), invest 100 percent of your Beating the Dow Asset Allocation portfolio in U.S. Treasury bills due to mature a year from now.

If the one-year change is on the negative side (*lower* than the year-ago price), invest 100 percent of your portfolio in the highest-yielding U.S. Government zero coupon bonds available that are due to mature in twenty years or more.

Figure 10.2 is an example of what your Asset Allocation Worksheet might look like after you've completed your research and made your calculations. The boldface numbers are fictional, gleaned from a January 1, 1999, edition of *Barron's* of my imagination, and provided for illustrative purposes only.

The results of this imaginary Asset Allocation Worksheet would show that from January 1, 1999 to January 1, 2000, you should invest 100 percent of your portfolio in the highest-yielding 20-year-plus U.S. Government zero coupon bonds available, rather than T-bills or stocks (see Figure 10.2).

1.	S&P Earnings Yield	4.25%
2.	10-Year U.S. Gov't T-bond Yield to Maturity	5.25%
3.		+ 0.30 %
4.	Estimated 10-Year AAA Corporate Bond Yield	5.55%
5.	[10-Year AAA Corporate Yield]	5.55%
	[Minus]	−
	[S&P Earnings Yield]	4.25%
6.	Last Week Gold Price Per Troy Ounce	306.90
7.	Year-Ago Gold Price Per Troy Ounce	339.65
8.	One-Year Change in Gold Price (Plus or Minus)	−32.75

Figure 10.2. Beating the Dow with T-bonds, T-bills, and Stocks
Asset Allocation Worksheet.

Step 17: Take Stock and Revamp

Sit back, relax, and do nothing but watch your returns come in for the next twelve months.

Then, on or about January first of next year, go out and buy *Barron's* again, and revisit your investment strategy by repeating Steps 3 through 17, making any changes in your portfolio deemed necessary by your latest research and calculations. Follow the same procedure every year thereafter.

And that's all there is, folks, to my new Beating the Dow with Bonds strategy. Told you I kept it simple!

ELEVEN

Getting Back into Stocks

This concluding chapter shows how to make winning stock portfolio selections using my Beating the Dow Five-Stock Strategy, provided that what you've learned following the formula in Chapter 10 has pointed to selecting stocks rather than T-bonds or T-bills as the optimal investment choice.

The Dow 30 Industrial Stocks

As I've stressed throughout this book, in the investment world, change is inevitable. Problems are inevitable. Companies are vulnerable, but the biggest of them have survivability. The best companies to invest in are those that know how to survive—namely the Dow 30 blue chips.

Here's a thumbnail history of each of today's Dow 30 stocks. There have been six substitutions (Caterpillar, Hewlett-Packard, Johnson & Johnson, J.P. Morgan, Wal-Mart, and Walt Disney) and one name change resulting from a merger, Primerica to The Travelers Group, since my first book was published, so I've pro-

171

filed these companies in a bit more detail. (For more in-depth information on the unchanged twenty-three, refer to *Beating the Dow: A High-Return, Low-Risk Method for Investing in the Dow 30 Industrial Stocks with as Little as $5,000*, published by Harper-Collins.)

AlliedSignal Inc. (ALD)

AlliedSignal was created in 1985 when Allied Corporation, formerly Allied Chemical, acquired the Signal Corporation, which was involved in oil and gas. In 1986, Allied spun off an assortment of these businesses, and now its annual sales of $12-plus billion stem from three sectors: aerospace (31 percent); automotive (31 percent); and engineered materials (38 percent), which include synthetic carpet fibers, solvents, and other items.

The aerospace sector, which derives about 55 percent of its revenues from commercial customers and the balance from government contracts, is the world's leading manufacturer of auxiliary power units for commercial transports and high-performance military aircraft, and of environmental control systems for all types of aircraft. It also leads the world in aircraft wheels and brakes. It is among the top producers of turboprop and turbofan engines used in the regional airliner and corporate jet markets.

AlliedSignal's automotive sector is the world's number one independent maker of passenger car and light truck brakes and components, turbochargers, and friction materials. It also makes safety restraints, filters, and spark plugs. It supplies both air and hydraulic drum and disc brakes and related components to the medium and heavy truck markets.

The engineered materials sector produces nylon and polyester carpet fibers, fluorine products, plastics, refrigerants and solvents, films, laminates, and other specialty products for markets ranging from home furnishings and packaging to electronics and telecommunications.

ALLIEDSIGNAL INC.

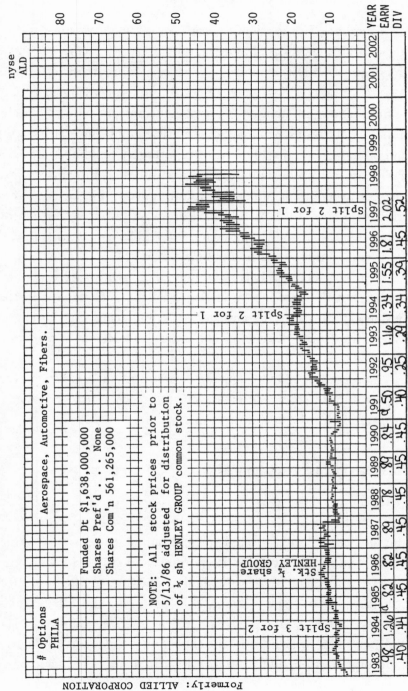

nyse
ALD

= Aerospace, Automotive, Fibers.

Options
PHILA

Funded Dt $1,638,000,000
Shares Pref'd . . . None
Shares Com'n 561,265,000

NOTE: All stock prices prior to
5/13/86 adjusted for distribution
of ¼ sh HENLEY GROUP common stock.

Split 2 for 1

Split 2 for 1

Stk. ¼ share
HENLEY GROUP

Split 3 for 2

Formerly: ALLIED CORPORATION

YEAR	1983	1984	1985	1986	1987	1988	1989	1990	1991	1992	1993	1994	1995	1996	1997	1998	1999	2000	2001	2002
EARN	d.98	1.26	d.82	.82	.80	.78	.89	.84	d.50	.95	1.16	1.34	1.55	1.81	2.02					
DIV	.40	.44	.45	.45	.45	.45	.45	.45	.40	.25	.29	.34	.39	.45	.52					

Aluminum Company of America/Alcoa (AA)

Aluminum Company of America has mining, refining, processing, fabricating, and selling locations in twenty countries, and is the world's largest aluminum producer. More than a third of Alcoa's average annual sales of $228.1 million are primary aluminum ingot and alumina. Twenty-eight percent of sales are aluminum and aluminum alloy that is fabricated into sheet, bars, wire, and other forms and sold to the transportation, building, industrial, and consumer products industries. End products range from various construction materials to aircraft. Alcoa's forged aluminum truck wheels lead the Australian, European, Japanese, and United States markets. About 30 percent of sales are sheet aluminum used for beverage and food cans and bottle caps.

Primarily because it is recyclable, aluminum is an expanding segment of the growing packaging industry, and Alcoa is in that business, too, with 1,600 affiliated recycling centers in the United States, the United Kingdom, and Australia. Alcoa is in plastics as well.

Aluminum is enjoying a boom period, and Alcoa is taking every opportunity to absorb costs and make its plants more efficient in preparation for the next downturn.

American Express Company (AXP)

Although most of us think of American Express as being exclusively in the credit card business ("You can't leave home without it"), this and other "travel-related services" amount to about one-third of the company's revenues. Its nontravel revenues derive from a variety of financial services, including Shearson Lehman Hutton, which American Express acquired in the 1980s and has expanded into the second-largest Wall Street firm after Merrill Lynch; IDS Financial Services, a huge financial planning, insurance, and mutual fund organization; and American Express Bank, Ltd., which pro-

ALCOA

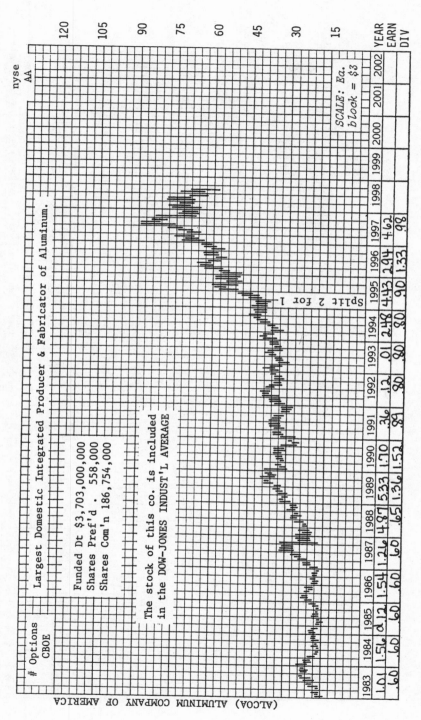

nyse
AA

Largest Domestic Integrated Producer & Fabricator of Aluminum.

Funded Dt $3,703,000,000
Shares Pref'd .   558,000
Shares Com'n 186,754,000

The stock of this co. is included
in the DOW-JONES INDUST'L AVERAGE

Options
CBOE

(ALCOA) ALUMINUM COMPANY OF AMERICA

SCALE: Ea.
block = $3

Split 2 for 1

YEAR	1983	1984	1985	1986	1987	1988	1989	1990	1991	1992	1993	1994	1995	1996	1997	1998	1999	2000	2001	2002
EARN	1.01	1.56	d.12	1.54	1.26	4.87	5.33	1.70	.36	.12	.01	2.48	4.43	2.04	4.62					
DIV	.60	.60	.60	.60	.60	.65	1.36	1.52	.89	.80	.80	.80	.90	1.33	.98					

AMERICAN EXPRESS COMPANY

nyse
AXP

SCALE: Ea.
block = $3

Travel Service, Insurance, Banking.

Funded Dt $7,832,000,000
Shares Pref'd . . . None
Shares Com'n 456,382,000

The stock of this co is included in the DOW-JONES IN-
DUSTRIAL AVERAGE.

Options
ASE, CBOE

Split 2 for 1

Split 3 for 2
Split 4 for 3

*LEHMAN stk dstr.

*All stock ranges prior 5/2/94
adjusted for stock dstr LEHMAN
BROS. HOLDINGS -- 1/5 share of
LEHMAN for ea. co. common sh.

YEAR	1983	1984	1985	1986	1987	1988	1989	1990	1991	1992	1993	1994	1995	1996	1997	1998	1999	2000	2001	2002
EARN	1.26	1.39	1.77	2.77	1.20	2.43	2.70	.69	1.59	.83	2.92	2.15	3.11	3.00	4.15					
DIV	.62	.64	.65	.68	.75	.76	.84	.92	.94	1.00	1.00	.95	.90	.90	.90					

Scale values: 120, 105, 90, 75, 60, 45, 30, 15

vides a range of banking services through one hundred offices in forty-three countries worldwide.

The Shearson unit, not alone among Wall Street firms, was beset with junk bond and bridge loan write-downs, bad loans, slow brokerage business, and massive layoffs in the 1980s. In June 1990, Shearson Lehman Hutton was restructured as two units: one, called Lehman Brothers (in a revival of one of the Street's most venerable names), is responsible for retail brokerage and money management activities.

A blue chip if ever there was one, American Express has annual revenues of $17.8 billion. Travel-related services account for 50 percent of the company's revenues; financial services, 22 percent; the American Express Bank, 5 percent; and other ventures (such as magazine publishing), 22 percent.

AT&T Corporation (T)

For many years, American Telephone & Telegraph Company, with a record of consistent dividends dating from 1881, was considered the premier "widows and orphans" stock. Although much has changed since the court-ordered breakup of Ma Bell in 1984, to this day more people own telephone stock than any other American equity investment.

AT&T has a profitable and expanding business base at home, what with its 1997 merger with another telecommunications giant, TCI; and a top-notch research and development capability in the inseparable and exciting areas of telecommunications and computer technology. Fiber optics have revolutionized home and office communications, and AT&T is intensely involved in critical areas of that technology. Unregulated overseas, it has the organizational as well as physical base to exploit opportunities both in products and services in Europe and elsewhere.

Though the company had a bumpy ride after its 1984 breakup, revenues today are in the $50-plus-billion range, the majority (59 percent) of sales coming from telecommunication services.

AT&T CORPORATION

nyse
T

SCALE: Ea. block = $2

Options CBOE

Communications Services, Equip't Leasing Business.

Funded Dt $6,008,000,000
Shares Pref'd . . . None
Shs Com'n 1,806,338,000

NOTE: Stock ranges prior 11/21/83 adjusted for spin off of seven regional baby Bells. Ranges prior 9/13/96 adjusted for spin off of LUCENT TECHNOLOGIES. Earnings and div's have not been adjusted.

The stock of this co. is included in the DOW-JONES INDUST'L AVERAGE.

Spin off .3 share LUCENT TECHNOLOGIES.

.0625 sh NCR CORP.

Formerly: AMERICAN TELEPHONE & TELEGRAPH CO.

YEAR	1982	1983	1984	1985	1986	1987	1988	1989	1990	1991	1992	1993	1994	1995	1996	1997	1998	1999	2000	2001
EARN	8.06	—	1.25	1.37	.21	1.88	4.55	2.50	2.40	.40	2.86	2.94	3.01	.09	3.66	2.84				
DIV	5.40	5.85	.90	1.20	1.20	1.20	1.20	1.20	1.29	1.32	1.32	1.32	1.32	1.32	1.32	1.32				

The Boeing Company (BA)

This aerospace giant was founded just before World War I by a lumber executive named William Boeing. During World War II, it was the leading producer of bombers, including the B-29 Super Fortress that dropped the Big One on Hiroshima and Nagasaki.

Boeing pioneered commercial jet aircraft; its 707, which could travel nonstop across the Atlantic for the first time, was used for the first scheduled passenger jet service flight in 1959, between New York and London.

The development in the early 1960s of quieter, more fuel-efficient, and far more powerful fan jet engines, led to the first Boeing 747 jumbo jet. But the 1970s saw a shape-up and shakeout in the airframe industry. Oil prices were on the rise again and the airlines began looking to replace their aging, narrow-body fleets with more fuel-efficient, wider-bodied jets. Boeing quickly established prominence with a $3-billion commitment to develop two midsized aircraft: a narrow-body 757 and a wide-body 767, each accommodating about two hundred passengers on trips of two thousand miles. Both met Federal Aviation Administration (FAA) requirements for extended-range operations, and the 767 exists in a model that can fly intercontinental routes. In the mid-1980s, oil prices plummeted, putting the carriers in a financial position to go ahead with long-delayed plans to modernize their fleets.

Today, aerospace is one of the few industries in which the United States still leads the world, and Boeing is the undisputed leader of the industry, having merged with the McDonnell Douglas Corporation in 1997. It has operations in 145 countries, twenty-seven U.S. states, and two Canadian provinces. Annual revenues average around $45 billion, the majority (87 percent) from commercial aircraft sales, mostly to Asia.

THE BOEING COMPANY

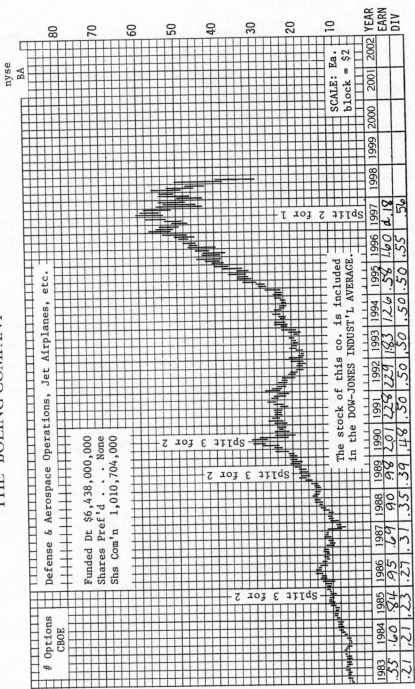

nyse
BA

Defense & Aerospace Operations, Jet Airplanes, etc.

Funded Dt $6,438,000,000
Shares Pref'd . . . None
Shs Com'n 1,010,704,000

Options
CBOE

Split 3 for 2

Split 3 for 2

Split 3 for 2

Split 3 for 2

Split 2 for 1

SCALE: Ea.
block = $2

The stock of this co. is included
in the DOW-JONES INDUST'L AVERAGE.

YEAR	1983	1984	1985	1986	1987	1988	1989	1990	1991	1992	1993	1994	1995	1996	1997	1998	1999	2000	2001	2002
EARN	.55	.60	.84	.95	.69	.90	.98	2.01	2.28	2.29	1.83	1.26.58	1.26.58	1.60	2.18					
DIV	.21	.21	.23	.27	.31	.35	.39	.48	.50	.50	.50	.50.50	.50.50	.55	.56					

Caterpillar Inc. (CAT)

When Californian Benjamin Holt modified the design of the traditional farm tractor in 1904, he had no idea where or how far his new concept in earthmoving equipment would take him. By using a gas engine instead of steam and replacing the tractor's wheels with crawler tracks, he distributed the weight of the vehicle more evenly. The vehicle was lighter and offered greater mobility than any other tractor on the market, able to inch swiftly through any and all types of soil, just like the caterpillar after which Holt had nicknamed his new contraption. Holt's modifications were so efficient, as well as durable, that the U.S. Army used the same design for its armored tanks during World War I.

With this success behind him, Holt quickly applied his ingenuity to developing other types of earthmoving equipment to be used in everything from road building to giant excavation and construction jobs. World War II enabled Holt to triple his sales and firmly establish his company as number one in the earthmoving machinery industry—well ahead of his closest competitor, International Harvester.

Sales grew steadily until about 1982, when competition from foreign firms, particularly in Japan, created major losses in market share for the company, ending fifty straight years of annually rising profits. But Caterpillar bounced back several years later when it shifted production to smaller equipment, reduced its workforce, and launched a multibillion-dollar effort to revitalize its manufacturing facilities here and abroad with automated "factory of the future" equipment.

Caterpillar entered the 1990s having regained its market share by doubling its product lines, which are sold under the names Caterpillar, Cat, Solar (a gas turbine engine manufacturer the company had bought in 1981), and Barber-Greene, an asphalt paving service it purchased in 1991. These products include: agricultural tractors and forest machines, backhoe loaders, diesel engines, exca-

CATERPILLAR INC.

Earth Moving Machinery: Diesel Engines.

Funded Dt $9,464,000,000
Shares Pref'd . . . None
Shares Com'n 364,754,000

nyse
CAT

Options
ASE

Formerly: CATERPILLAR TRACTOR CO.

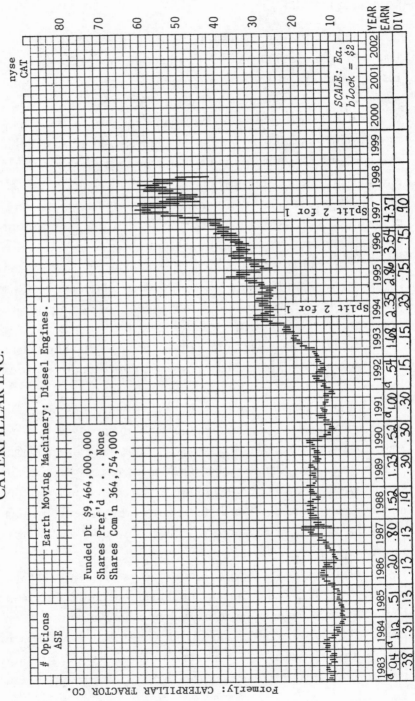

SCALE: Ea.
block = $2

Split 2 for 1

Split 2 for 1

	1983	1984	1985	1986	1987	1988	1989	1990	1991	1992	1993	1994	1995	1996	1997	1998	1999	2000	2001	2002	YEAR
	d.94	d1.12	.51	.20	.80	1.52	1.23	.52	d1.00	d.54	1.68	2.35	2.86	3.54	4.37						EARN
	.38	.31	.13	.13	.13	.19	.30	.30	.30	.15	.15	.23	.75	.75	.90						DIV

vators, lift trucks, loaders, log skidders, materials-handling vehicles, motor graders, paving products, pipe layers, power generation systems, scrapers, spark-ignited engines, tractors, and turbine engines.

Caterpillar also entered that decade under a cloud of negative publicity when UAW workers struck the company and were seen protesting their wages, health care, plant relocations, and other grievances on the nightly news for more than a year, causing sales to drop by 11 percent.

The company and its union workers never came to bargaining terms, as contract talks ground to a permanent halt; most of the company's workers went back on the job, but they've been working without a union contract ever since.

The company recouped its losses, and sales have climbed continually skyward throughout the decade as Caterpillar has expanded its joint venture and overseas activities, particularly in China.

Today, the Illinois-based manufacturer has completely regained its position as the world's premier producer of top-quality earth-moving equipment; it is also the number one maker of gas turbine engines for industrial applications. It offers financing and related services as well through its Caterpillar Financial Services Corporation and Caterpillar Insurance Company Ltd. components.

With forty-one plants in twelve countries and independent dealerships in 127 countries, Caterpillar's annual sales are $18.9 billion, broken down as follows: machinery, 61 percent; engines, 32 percent; and financial services, 7 percent.

Chevron Corporation (CHV)

Oil is the source of energy that powers our transportation, heats our homes and businesses, runs the generators that turn on our lights, and is the raw material for many of our key industries, such as chemicals, textiles, drugs, and plastics.

CHEVRON CORPORATION

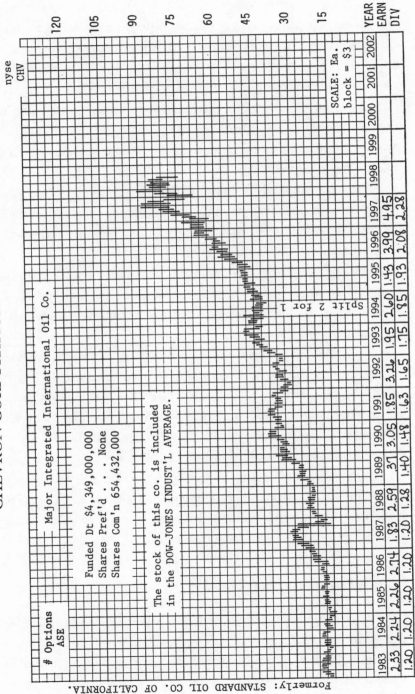

nyse
CHV

Major Integrated International Oil Co.

Funded Dt $4,349,000,000
Shares Pref'd . . . None
Shares Com'n 654,432,000

The stock of this co. is included
in the DOW-JONES INDUST'L AVERAGE.

Options
ASE

Formerly: STANDARD OIL CO. OF CALIFORNIA.

SCALE: Ea.
block = $3

Split 2 for 1

YEAR	1983	1984	1985	1986	1987	1988	1989	1990	1991	1992	1993	1994	1995	1996	1997	1998	1999	2000	2001	2002
EARN	2.33	2.24	2.26	2.74	1.83	2.59	.37	3.05	1.85	3.26	1.95	2.60	1.43	3.99	4.95					
DIV	1.20	1.20	1.20	1.20	1.20	1.28	1.40	1.48	1.63	1.65	1.75	1.85	1.93	1.08	2.28					

But the supply is limited to discovered reserves and by the technology used to exploit them. While the long-term demand for oil as an energy source is steadily growing, supply is steadily diminishing, and I foresee nothing on the technological horizon to change that.

When oil prices are low, companies typically cut back on exploration and drilling, which means that when prices go back up again, those companies with big reserves are in a better position to prosper.

Chevron has sizable reserves. It has long been committed to a major asset-restructuring plan involving the sale of unprofitable units and the upgrading of existing exploration production facilities. And its acquisitions of Gulf and Tenneco's natural gas properties in Mexico have added to its sound shape.

Although Chevron's core market continues to be Southern California, it is ranked number three among U.S. oil companies. Ninety percent of its annual revenues of $40.6 billion derive from petroleum.

The Coca-Cola Company (KO)

It's quite likely—indeed, probable—that there is no one in the civilized world who hasn't heard of Coca-Cola, a brand name that has become synonymous with almost anything that is popular and ubiquitous. Today, Coca-Cola, which operates in more than 160 countries, has 45 percent of the global market for soft drink sales, more than double the share of any competitor.

The company has also ventured into diversification, with its 1977 acquisition of Taylor Wines (sold to Seagram in 1983) and its purchase of 49 percent of Columbia Pictures (sold to Sony in 1989), profitable investments both. In 1986, the company created a new corporation, Coca-Cola Enterprises (CCE), Inc., to own its largest bottlers. CCE issued stock publicly; the Coca-Cola Company owns about 49 percent of CCE, which is separately listed on the New York Stock Exchange.

THE COCA-COLA COMPANY

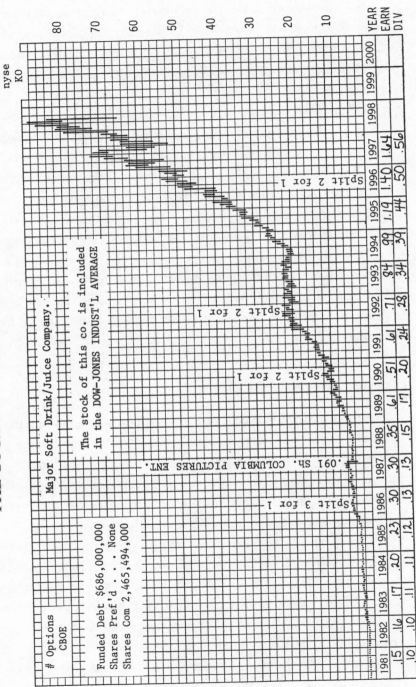

nyse
KO

Options
CBOE

Major Soft Drink/Juice Company.

The stock of this co. is included
in the DOW-JONES INDUST'L AVERAGE

Funded Debt $686,000,000
Shares Pref'd . . . None
Shares Com 2,465,494,000

Split 2 for 1

Split 2 for 1

Split 2 for 1

Split 3 for 1

091 Sh. COLUMBIA PICTURES ENT.

YEAR	1981	1982	1983	1984	1985	1986	1987	1988	1989	1990	1991	1992	1993	1994	1995	1996	1997	1998	1999	2000
EARN	.15	.16	.17	.20	.23	.30	.30	.35	.61	.51	.61	.71	.84	.99	1.19	1.40	1.64			
DIV	.10	.10	.11	.11	.12	.13	.13	.15	.17	.20	.24	.28	.34	.39	.44	.50	.56			

In the 1980s, Coca-Cola's sales increased by almost 75 percent, and earnings per share tripled. In the 1990s, revenues have climbed to $18.9 billion a year, 96 percent of them from soft drink sales. It's a fabulous company, and the market knows it. Like the market in general, its stock is now quite expensive, with a low yield and a high price to earnings ratio.

E.I. du Pont de Nemours and Company (DD)

When du Pont introduced women's nylon stockings in 1940, it sold 64 million pair the first year. That was the beginning of this one-time maker of gunpowder's preeminence in the manufacture of artificial fibers made from petrochemicals, which dominated the textile and apparel industries until the mid-1970s, when natural fibers made a comeback.

Pierre du Pont, who with his cousins bought the company from the family in 1902, revolutionized corporate finance accounting and budgeting techniques, and has been called the "architect of the modern corporation." A still widely used technique for calculating return on assets is known as the du Pont Formula.

Pierre also got the company to buy, cheaply, 28 percent of the young General Motors, and he hired Alfred P. Sloan to build it into the world's largest industrial corporation. In 1981, in what was the largest business transaction in history up to that time, du Pont broke up a fight for Continental Oil Company involving Seagram Distillers, Dome Petroleum, and Mobil, paying $7.2 billion for the oil giant and assuring a source of raw materials.

Today, with operations in seventy countries and nearly 45 percent of its sales generated outside the United States, du Pont derives the majority of its average annual sales of $45.1 billion from oil and energy-related businesses; 39 percent from industrial and consumer chemical products, fibers, and polymers; and the

E.I. du PONT de NEMOURS AND COMPANY

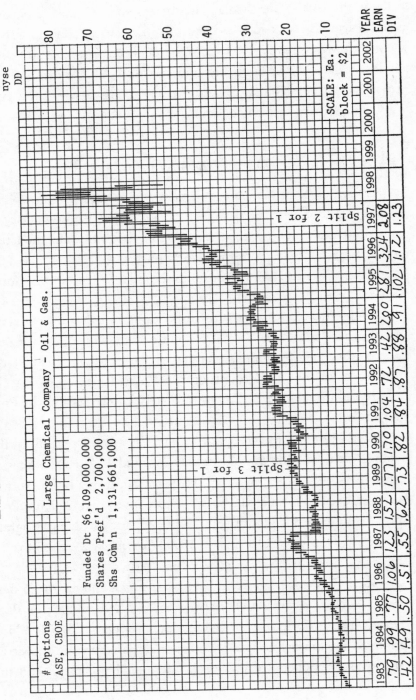

nyse DD

Large Chemical Company – Oil & Gas.

Funded Dt $6,109,000,000
Shares Pref'd 2,700,000
Shs Com'n 1,131,661,000

Options
ASE, CBOE

SCALE: Ea.
block = $2

Split 2 for 1

Split 3 for 1

YEAR	1983	1984	1985	1986	1987	1988	1989	1990	1991	1992	1993	1994	1995	1996	1997	1998	1999	2000	2001	2002
EARN	.79	.99	.77	1.06	1.23	1.52	1.77	1.70	1.04	.72	.42	2.90	2.81	3.24	2.08					
DIV	.42	.49	.50	.51	.55	.62	.73	.82	.84	.87	.88	.91	1.02	1.12	1.23					

balance from a group of diversified businesses ranging from agricultural products to sporting goods, medical products, and pharmaceuticals.

Eastman Kodak Company (EK)

George Eastman founded this company more than a century ago, adding to the name the word Kodak—which is not a misspelling of the Alaskan bear, but a coined word—simply because he liked the letter K.

Today, Eastman Kodak's sales stem from three areas: imaging (cameras, film, processing services, and related supplies), approximately 54 percent; information (office copiers, electronic equipment, and related products), approximately 9 percent; and health (Sterling Drugs, Lehn & Fink Products), 37 percent.

The Health Division, which features some leading specialized pharmaceutical products, like analgesics, and such well-known Lehn & Fink products as Lysol disinfectant, has combined Sterling Drug's strength in health products with Kodak's imaging capabilities. The company sees its future coming from research and development in diagnostic imaging, cardiovascular medicine, oncology, viral diseases, and central nervous system disorders.

In 1989, Kodak underwent some $875 million in restructuring costs. At the same time, it invested more than $2 billion in capital improvements, including a new research center for Sterling to bolster the ethical drug segment of its business. In total, it spent $1.25 billion on research and development benefiting all four of Kodak's business sectors.

Forty-five percent of Kodak's $14.5 billion annual revenues come from outside the United States, making the company global but vulnerable to weak foreign currencies. Institutional investors hold only 48 percent of its stock, compared with a more typical 65 or 70 percent for Dow stocks in general.

EASTMAN KODAK COMPANY

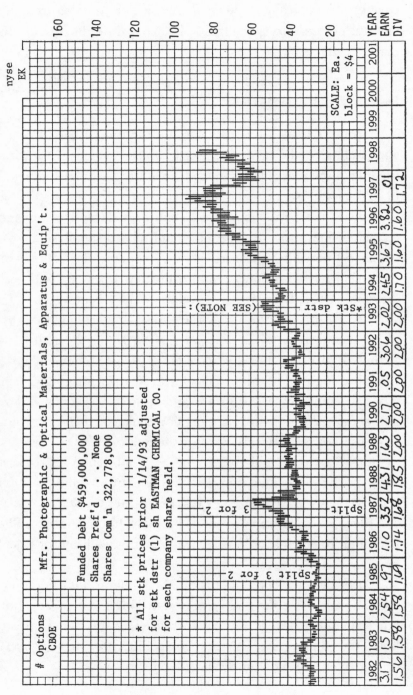

nyse

EK

Mfr. Photographic & Optical Materials, Apparatus & Equip't.

Options
CBOE

Funded Debt $459,000,000
Shares Pref'd . . . None
Shares Com'n 322,778,000

* All stk prices prior 1/14/93 adjusted
for stk dstr (1) sh EASTMAN CHEMICAL CO.
for each company share held.

SCALE: Ea.
block = $4

Split 3 for 2

3 for 2
Split

*Stk dstr -   :(SEE NOTE)

YEAR	1982	1983	1984	1985	1986	1987	1988	1989	1990	1991	1992	1993	1994	1995	1996	1997	1998	1999	2000	2001
EARN	3.17	1.51	2.54	.97	1.10	3.52	4.31	1.63	2.17	.05	3.06	2.02	2.45	3.67	3.82	.01				
DIV	1.56	1.58	1.58	1.60	1.74	1.68	1.85	2.00	2.00	2.00	2.00	2.00	1.70	1.60	1.60	1.72				

Exxon Corporation (XON)

Exxon is the world's largest oil company and third-largest industrial corporation. With record 1997 earnings of $8.5 billion, the highest of any company in the world, its activities range from exploration to transportation and marketing. It has operations in the United States and more than eighty countries worldwide, and is a major producer of coal and manufacturer of petrochemicals, too.

Except for an ill-fated but relatively inexpensive ($1.2 billion) acquisition of Reliance Electric in 1979, Exxon has used its prosperity to improve its position in the energy field rather than diversify. In 1989, through its 70 percent–owned Canadian subsidiary Imperial Oil, Exxon bought Texaco Canada for approximately $4.1 billion, adding significantly to its already vast reserves of oil and natural gas.

In recent years, it has been using its profits after dividends to buy back its own stock, adding a boost to the market value of the remaining holdings. Revenues are in excess of $117.6 billion a year.

Despite its public relations fiasco in 1989 when the tanker *Exxon Valdez* ran aground in Alaska's Prince William Sound, Exxon is not simply a great oil company, but one of the greatest companies of any kind in the world.

General Electric Company (GE)

GE is an octopus among corporations, with tentacles reaching everywhere. It has approximately 146 manufacturing plants in thirty U.S. states and Puerto Rico, and 114 plants in twenty-four other countries. Its average annual revenues of $89.3 billion account for almost 2 percent of the entire U.S. gross national product.

Its numerous sectors have shown the following approximate contributions to revenues in the 1990s: capital services (equipment management, specialty insurance, consumer services, specialized

EXXON CORPORATION

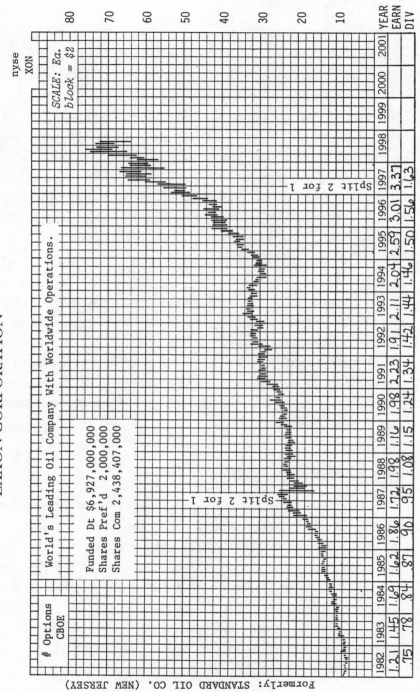

nyse
XON

SCALE: Ea.
block = $2

Options
CBOE

World's Leading Oil Company With Worldwide Operations.

Funded Dt $6,927,000,000
Shares Pref'd 2,000,000
Shares Com 2,438,407,000

Split 2 for 1

Split 2 for 1

Formerly: STANDARD OIL CO. (NEW JERSEY)

YEAR	1982	1983	1984	1985	1986	1987	1988	1989	1990	1991	1992	1993	1994	1995	1996	1997	1998	1999	2000	2001
EARN	1.21	1.45	1.69	1.62	1.86	1.72	1.98	1.16	1.98	2.23	1.91	2.11	2.04	2.59	3.01	3.37				
DIV	.75	.78	.84	.87	.90	.95	1.08	1.15	1.24	1.34	1.42	1.44	1.46	1.50	1.56	1.63				

GENERAL ELECTRIC COMPANY

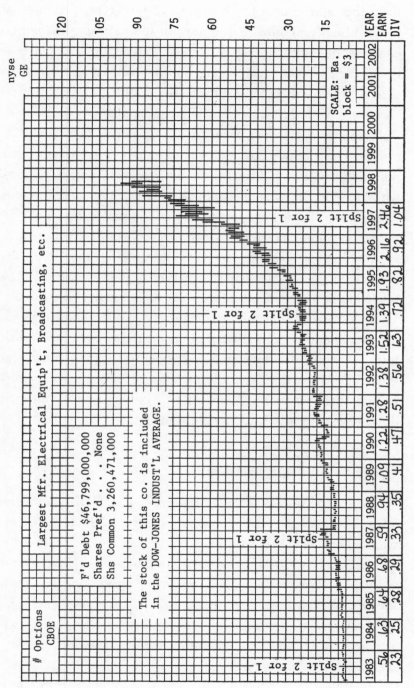

nyse
GE

Largest Mfr. Electrical Equip't, Broadcasting, etc.

Options
CBOE

F'd Debt $46,799,000,000
Shares Pref'd . . . None
Shs Common 3,260,471,000

The stock of this co. is included
in the DOW-JONES INDUST'L AVERAGE.

SCALE: Ea.
block = $3

Split 2 for 1
Split 2 for 1
Split 2 for 1
Split 2 for 1

YEAR	1983	1984	1985	1986	1987	1988	1989	1990	1991	1992	1993	1994	1995	1996	1997	1998	1999	2000	2001	2002
EARN	.56	.63	.64	.68	.59	.94	1.09	1.22	1.28	1.38	1.52	1.39	1.93	2.16	2.46					
DIV	.23	.25	.28	.29	.33	.35	.41	.47	.51	.56	.63	.72	.82	.92	1.04					

financing, and midmarket financing), 24 percent; materials (silicones, Lexan, and other plastics used in automotive, packaging, and construction industries), 18 percent; aircraft engines (which are sold to Boeing and other commercial and military aerospace manufacturers), 9 percent; broadcasting (NBC, CNBC, and MSNBC, its coventure with Microsoft), 3 percent; appliances (refrigerators, dishwashers, microwave ovens, etc.), 4 percent; lighting systems, electrical distribution and control, industrial control systems, transportation services (lightbulbs, circuit breakers, motors for BMW windows, locomotives, and mining vehicles), 19 percent; medical systems, information services (X-ray and ultrasound systems, computer and communications systems and services), 14 percent; power systems (gas and steam turbine generators), 9 percent.

Prior to the 1980s, when Jack Welch took over as CEO, GE tended to be a cyclical rather than a steady growth stock. But under Welch's "lean and mean" management style, the company's focus on consolidation, diversification, decentralization, cost cutting, quality customer service, and component strength—emphasizing those businesses that have the capacity be either number one or two in their respective fields, and divesting itself of those that don't—the company has truly blossomed.

General Motors Corporation (GM)

GM is the world's largest corporation; its $177.7 billion annual sales are approximately 3 percent of the United States gross national product.

Although it is best known as an automaker, GM is much more than that. General Motors Acceptance Corporation (GMAC) is the world's largest finance company, and GM makes trucks, giant locomotives, military vehicles, radar and weapons systems, as well as computer chips, satellite communications networks, and information systems and services.

In 1984, GM paid $2.6 billion for Ross Perot's Electronic Data

GENERAL MOTORS CORPORATION

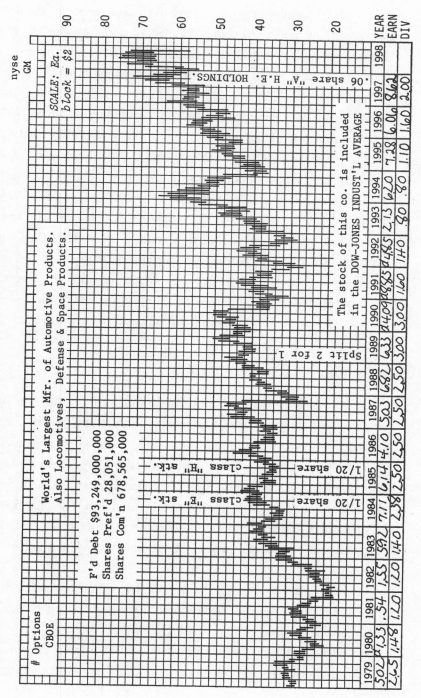

nyse
GM

SCALE: Ea.
block = $2

World's Largest Mfr. of Automotive Products.
Also Locomotives, Defense & Space Products.

F'd Debt $93,249,000,000
Shares Pref'd 28,051,000
Shares Com'n 678,565,000

The stock of this co. is included
in the DOW-JONES INDUST'L AVERAGE

Split 2 for 1

Class "H" stk. —— 1/20 share

Class "E" stk. —— 1/20 share

.06 share "A" H.E. HOLDINGS.

Options
CBOE

YEAR	1979	1980	1981	1982	1983	1984	1985	1986	1987	1988	1989	1990	1991	1992	1993	1994	1995	1996	1997	1998
EARN	5.02	1.33	.54	1.55	5.92	7.11	6.14	4.10	5.03	6.82	6.33	d4.09	d8.85	d4.85	2.13	6.20	7.28	6.06	8.62	
DIV	2.65	1.48	1.20	1.20	1.40	2.38	2.50	2.50	2.50	2.50	3.00	3.00	1.60	1.40	.80	.80	1.10	1.60	2.00	

90
80
70
60
50
40
30
20

Systems (EDS), the biggest company in the fast-growing data processing systems field. GM also has a class of common shares, called Series E, which are separately traded and receive an earmarked flow of dividends, based on a specified percentage of EDS profits.

Also in 1984, GM acquired Hughes Aircraft Corporation, a defense electronics giant, for $5 billion, combined it with the existing operations of Delco Electronics under a newly formed GM Hughes Electronics Corporation (GMHE) banner, and created another separate class of common shares, called Series H.

GM's stock sold cheap in the early 1990s because of the company's mixed performance in the previous decade, and the economy's effect on auto sales. But new management embarked on a strenuous cost-cutting campaign, including plant closings and staff cuts (that led to some costly labor strikes), put out some exciting new models, and the company has regained its lost market share, with 90 percent of sales coming from its automotive products.

Goodyear Tire & Rubber Company (GT)

Goodyear is the world's largest producer of rubber and this country's biggest tire maker, with thirty-three plants in the United States and thirty-nine others in more than twenty-five countries.

Virtually all the important American tire manufacturers except Goodyear have been bought up by foreign companies. Goodyear itself fell prey to a takeover attempt in 1986 by international predator Sir James Goldsmith, but the takeover was successfully thwarted. However, the company's balance sheet was badly wounded in the process.

Profitability was further hampered by an unsuccessful foray into the oil business in the 1980s that left Goodyear's earnings off 41 percent by the end of the decade.

About 85 percent of Goodyear's sales derive from automotive products, mainly tires, but also hoses, belts, tubes, foam cushioning accessories, and repair services. Most of the balance is from the

GOODYEAR TIRE & RUBBER COMPANY

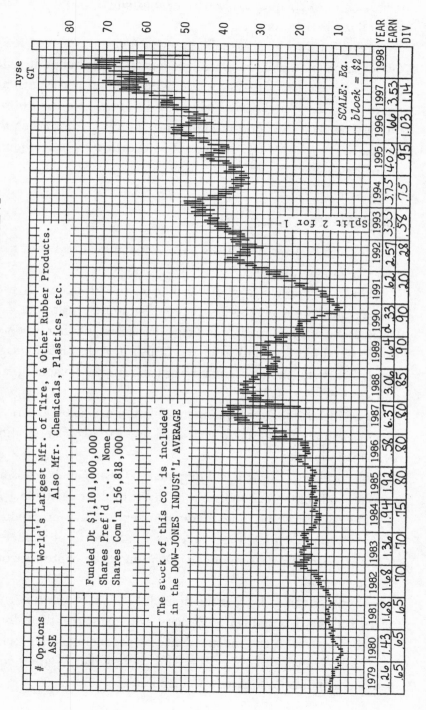

nyse
GT

Options
ASE

World's Largest Mfr. of Tire, & Other Rubber Products.
Also Mfr. Chemicals, Plastics, etc.

Funded Dt $1,101,000,000
Shares Pref'd . . . None
Shares Com'n 156,818,000

The stock of this co. is included
in the DOW-JONES INDUST'L AVERAGE

Split 2 for 1

SCALE: Ea.
block = $2

	1979	1980	1981	1982	1983	1984	1985	1986	1987	1988	1989	1990	1991	1992	1993	1994	1995	1996	1997	1998	YEAR
	1.26	1.43	1.68	1.68	1.36	1.94	1.92	.58	6.37	3.06	1.64	d.33	.62	2.57	3.33	3.75	4.02	.66	3.53		EARN
	.65	.65	.65	.70	.70	.75	.80	.80	.80	.85	.90	.90	.20	.28	.58	.75	.95	1.03	1.14		DIV

manufacture of chemicals, plastics, shoe products, roofing materials, and industrial products.

A cyclical stock that has fallen prey at times to recession fears, Goodyear is another Dow stock that has taken its lumps at times and sold relatively cheap. But it has invested in modern plants, has restructured itself organizationally, and has largely rid itself of the oil business so it can concentrate on making tires, from which the company derives about 75 percent of its approximately $12 billion annual sales.

Hewlett-Packard Company (HWP)

Hewlett-Packard derives its $42 billion annual revenues from four component divisions.

The Computer Systems and Peripheral Products Division makes calculators, computers (laptop, multiuser, palmtop, personal, and workstation), disk and tape drives, networking products, printers and plotters, and scanners. It also provides data management, distributed systems, and network and software planning sales and services.

The Electronic Test Equipment Division produces an array of diagnostic and measurement gear used in a variety of applications by many industries.

The Medical Electronic Equipment Division makes hospital supplies and computer software used in the health care field.

The Analytical Instrumentation and Service Division produces chromatographs, mass spectrometers, and spectrophotometers. And the Electronic Components Division makes optoelectronic devices and video servers.

All this began in 1938 as the brainchild of two California engineers, Bill Hewlett and David Packard, who made real their dream of achieving wealth and independence by producing audio oscillators on their own time in a Palo Alto garage, the fledgling company's combined headquarters and laboratory.

Disney Studios in Burbank helped them on their road to success by purchasing a number of the duo's expensive oscillators for
use in the production of Disney's animated paean to classical
music, *Fantasia* (1940).

Increased demand for Hewlett-Packard's electronic testing
equipment spawned by America's entry into World War II a year
later took the company's revenues to the stratospheric $1 million
mark by 1943, considerably boosting Hewlett-Packard's fortunes
and capabilities for expansion. Growing at the astonishing rate of
50 percent to 100 percent each year, Hewlett-Packard had, by the
close of the decade, branched out into a wide range of activities via
European subsidiaries and a bold strategy of ever increasing acquisition.

The company entered the medical equipment field in 1961 by
purchasing the Sanborn Company, and moved into analytical
instrumentation four years later with its addition of F&M
Scientific. The 1970s saw Hewlett-Packard become a pioneer in
the emerging field of personal computing with its introduction of
the HP-35, a handheld scientific calculator. By the end of the
decade, virtually half the company's earnings derived from sales of
computer and related equipment. It continued its record of success
in the computer field into the 1990s with its introduction of the
HP-85 personal computer, the HP-9000 desktop mainframe, the
laser printer, and a host of other computer and calculator-related
products and services.

By the time David Packard retired in 1993 (Bill Hewlett had
retired in 1987), however, the company was forced to make some
significant changes due to a flattening out of growth in market
share stemming from heated competition in the computer industry.
The company has since converted its laser printers to more
advanced and efficient LaserJet models, changed over its microwave component technology to video, upgraded most of its other
products and services, and formed several partnerships to reduce
production time.

HEWLETT-PACKARD COMPANY

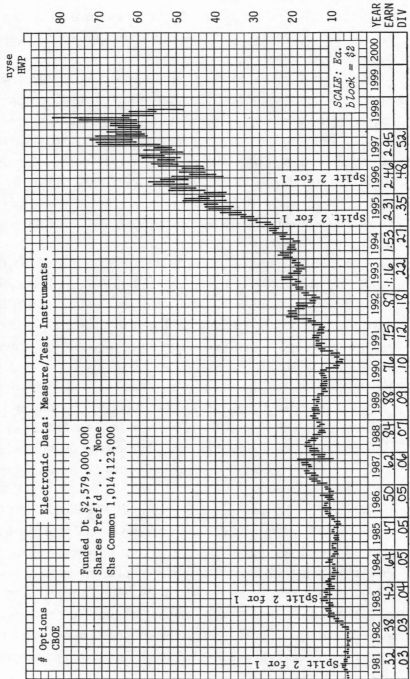

nyse
HWP

Electronic Data: Measure/Test Instruments.

Options
CBOE

Funded Dt $2,579,000,000
Shares Pref'd . . . None
Shs Common 1,014,123,000

SCALE: Ea.
block = $2

YEAR	1981	1982	1983	1984	1985	1986	1987	1988	1989	1990	1991	1992	1993	1994	1995	1996	1997	1998	1999	2000
EARN	.32	.38	.42	.64	.47	.50	.62	.84	.88	.76	.75	.87	1.16	1.53	2.31	2.46	2.95			
DIV	.03	.03	.04	.05	.05	.05	.06	.07	.09	.10	.12	.18	.22	.27	.35	.48	.52			

Split 2 for 1
Split 2 for 1
Split 2 for 1
Split 2 for 1

Hewlett-Packard has product manufacturing and development operations in nine states, Puerto Rico, and sixteen countries that are supported by 600 sales and service offices in 110 countries worldwide. Its Computer Systems and Peripheral Products Division continues to be the company's biggest income producer, accounting for 77 percent of annual revenues. The Electronic Test Equipment sector comes in a distant second at 11 percent. The Medical Electronic Equipment Division generates 6 percent of sales, while the Analytical Instrumentation and Electronic Components sectors contribute revenues of 3 percent each.

Hewlett-Packard's continued efforts to keep up with the times (and stay just little bit ahead of them) in the field of computers—which is virtually characterized by instant obsolescence—as well as its streamlining of expenses (the company has reduced its acquisition spending from $423 million to $93 million), plus its vast inventory will, management hopes, be reflected in increasingly higher profits every year well into the next century. And as the nineties draw to an end, those hopes have so far been right on the money.

International Business Machines Corporation (IBM)

IBM led America into the computer age, and for many years *was* the computer industry.

In the 1960s, IBM developed its 360 series of huge "mainframe" computers designed for any kind of data processing need. Soon after its debut, the 360 established IBM's market dominance, its power to set industry standards and compete for new business, thus catching the attention of the Department of Justice. An antitrust suit, filed in 1969, hung over IBM like an ominous cloud until it was dropped in the early 1980s.

In the 1970s, independent firms began undermining IBM's

INTERNATIONAL BUSINESS MACHINES CORPORATION

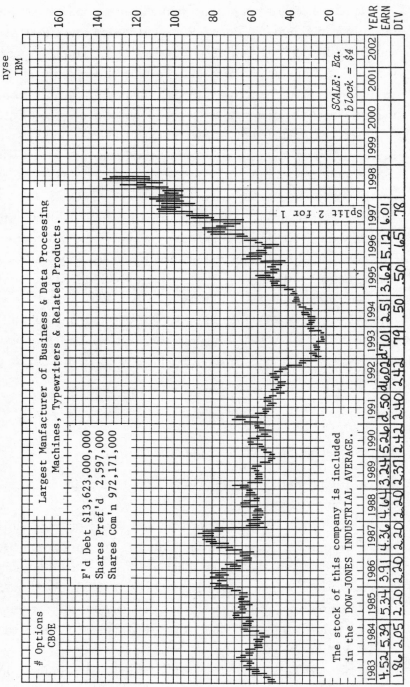

nyse
IBM

Options
CBOE

Largest Manfacturer of Business & Data Processing
Machines, Typewriters & Related Products.

F'd Debt $13,623,000,000
Shares Pref'd 2,597,000
Shares Com'n 972,171,000

Split 2 for 1

SCALE: Ea.
block = $4

The stock of this company is included
in the DOW-JONES INDUSTRIAL AVERAGE.

YEAR	1983	1984	1985	1986	1987	1988	1989	1990	1991	1992	1993	1994	1995	1996	1997	1998	1999	2000	2001	2002
EARN	4.52	5.39	5.34	3.91	4.36	4.44	3.24	5.26	d.50	d6.02	d7.01	2.51	3.62	5.12	6.01					
DIV	1.84	2.05	2.20	2.20	2.20	2.30	2.37	2.42	2.42	2.42	.79	.50	.50	.65	.78					

mainframe leasing business by offering lower rental rates, while others began to bring on the clones—IBM-compatible peripheral equipment that sold at prices cheaper than IBM's. But the biggest blow to IBM's dominance was the development of the minicomputer industry, featuring smaller, more flexible systems that companies could more easily adapt to their particular needs. IBM stood on the dock as the minicomputer boat sailed away, and saw its market share drop from 60 percent to 40 percent.

Determined not to miss the next boat—home microcomputers for data processing and entertainment—IBM introduced the PC (personal computer) in 1981. Despite heightened competition and price wars, it continued to dominate, but with reduced market share, into the mid-1980s, a time of slackened growth in the computer industry generally. IBM was the biggest loser, but it has bounced back with sales in excess of $60 billion, and for the most part, has kept right on sailing.

International Paper Company (IP)

International Paper Company is the world's largest producer of packaging, printing, and writing papers, as well as corrugated boxes, photographic papers and films, and lumber and wood products. Through outlets in more than 130 countries, it distributes paper and building materials mainly manufactured by others. It is also involved in oil and gas exploration and drilling through royalty arrangements with oil companies, and is engaged in real estate activities as well.

Approximately 60 percent of International Paper's annual sales of $20.1 billion are equally divided between pulp and paper, paperboard, and packaging. About 7 percent derives from distribution activities, and the balance from wood products, timber, and specialty products.

Paper is a cyclical business that waxes and wanes with the

INTERNATIONAL PAPER COMPANY

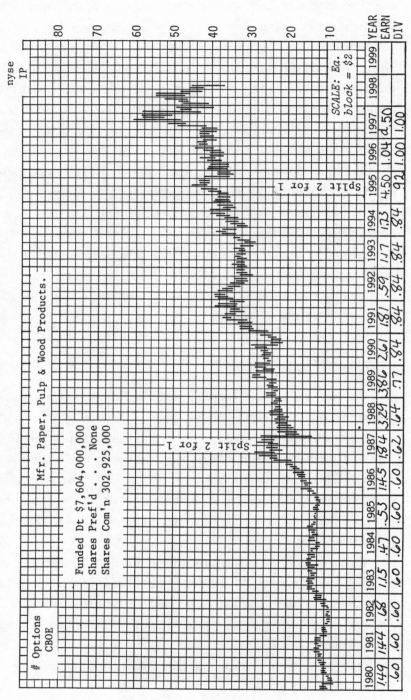

nyse
IP

Mfr. Paper, Pulp & Wood Products.

\# Options
CBOE

Funded Dt $7,604,000,000
Shares Pref'd . . . None
Shares Com'n 302,925,000

SCALE: Ea.
block = $2

Split 2 for 1

Split 2 for 1

YEAR	1980	1981	1982	1983	1984	1985	1986	1987	1988	1989	1990	1991	1992	1993	1994	1995	1996	1997	1998	1999
EARN	1.49	1.44	.68	1.15	.47	.53	1.45	1.84	3.24	3.86	2.61	1.81	.59	1.17	1.73	4.50	1.04	2.50		
DIV	.60	.60	.60	.60	.60	.60	.60	.62	.64	.77	.84	.84	.84	.84	.84	.921	1.00	1.00		

economy generally and the construction sector specifically. But it is also a growth business, tied to worldwide literacy and also to economic activity. Today's concerns about the environment are likely to continue into the next century as well, and this will serve to favor the paper packaging industry over nonbiodegradable plastics.

It is an industry in which technology plays an important role, and International Paper has invested billions of dollars to make itself one of the lowest-cost producers in each of its market sectors.

The company has production operations in twenty-six countries, and has the technology and the market position to continue to dominate in an industry that should enjoy global growth in the twenty-first century.

Johnson & Johnson (JNJ)

Johnson & Johnson is second only to Merck (another Dow 30 component) as the world's leading manufacturer of health care products for personal and medical industry use. The company's product lines fall within three sectors: consumer products, professional products, and pharmaceutical products.

Johnson & Johnson's brand name consumer products include: Acuvue contact lenses, Baby Oil, Baby Shampoo, Band-Aids, Clean & Clear (for skin care), Imodium A-D (an antidiarrhea medicine), Monistat 7 (for treating yeast infection), Mylanta antacid, Reach toothbrushes, Serenity incontinence products, and Tylenol pain reliever.

Its line of professional products includes: Hepatitis C testing systems, joint replacement items, and surgical instruments.

Brand name pharmaceuticals include: Duragesic (an analgesic), Eprex (an antianemia agent), Ergamisol (for cancer treatment), the antibacterial Floxin, Hismanal (an antihistamine), Nizoral (an antifungus treatment), Ortho-Novum (for birth control), Prepulsid (a digestive aid), and the acne cream Retin-A.

The medical products giant was created in 1885 by two Johnson brothers, James and Edward. A third brother, Robert, joined the team in 1886; that year the company's product line was expanded to include antiseptic surgical dressings. This addition led to the development in 1921 of that staple first aid product found in every household, the Band-Aid. Another staple was introduced the same year, Johnson & Johnson's Baby Oil.

As the nineteenth century drew to a close, brother Edward left the company to form his own medical products firm (which years later was folded into Bristol-Myers Squibb), leaving just two Johnsons at the helm once again.

Over the years, James and Robert (and subsequently, Robert Jr.) continued to grow the company's offerings by moving into many other areas of health care, including birth control products and sutures. They also began acquiring other companies, such as McNeil Labs, developers of the nonaspirin pain reliever Tylenol. With the purchase of Iolab Corporation in 1980, the company entered the field of cataract surgery with its development of interocular lenses. The purchase of Lifescan in 1986 gave Johnson & Johnson a line of glucose monitoring systems for diabetics.

By the 1980s, the company's overall sales were in the neighborhood of $5 billion annually, money that it continued to pour into the research and development of a seemingly never-ending stream of new products such as Acuvue, the first disposable contact lens, and Retin-A for skin treatment.

This amazing record of success experienced its only major setbacks during the same decade, however. The first came when Johnson & Johnson's arthritic pain reliever Zomax was tied to several deaths, and the product had to be shelved. The second, more severe, and most notorious, blow to the company's fortunes occurred in 1982 when eight individuals succumbed from consuming capsules of Johnson & Johnson's popular acetaminophen Tylenol that had been laced with cyanide by person or persons

JOHNSON & JOHNSON

nyse
JNJ

Options
CBOE

Health Care Products: Drugs, Surgical Dressings, etc.

Funded Dt $1,126,000,000
Shares Pref'd ... None
Shs Common 1,346,455,000

SCALE: Ea.
block = $2

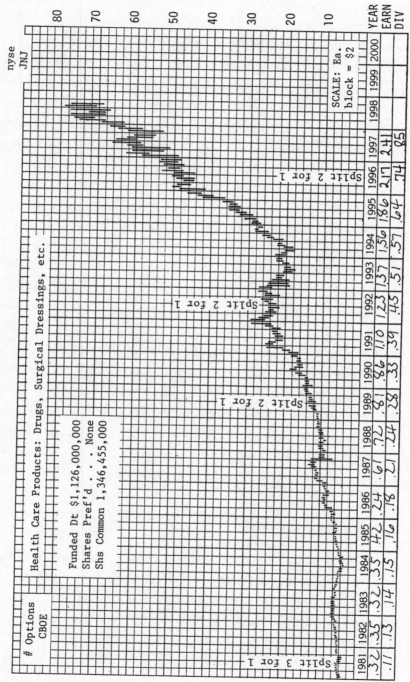

Split 2 for 1.
Split 2 for 1.
Split 2 for 1.
Split 3 for 1.

YEAR	1981	1982	1983	1984	1985	1986	1987	1988	1989	1990	1991	1992	1993	1994	1995	1996	1997	1998	1999	2000
EARN	.32	.35	.32	.35	.42	.24	.61	.72	.81	.86	1.10	1.23	1.37	1.56	1.86	2.17	2.41			
DIV	.11	.13	.14	.15	.16	.18	.21	.24	.28	.33	.39	.45	.51	.57	.64	.74	.85			

unknown. The perpetrator was never caught. Sales of Tylenol plummeted 50 percent as 31 million bottles of the over-the-counter medicine were pulled from store shelves by the company and checked for tampering. The "Tylenol Scare" that followed as a result of the eight unfortunate deaths and the massive recall cost the company $240 million. Nevertheless, the scare did have its upside. It resulted in the creation of safer, tamper-proof packaging not only for Tylenol, which the company rescued from going under due to its forthrightness in dealing with the scare, but many other products in and out of the health care field. Today, Tylenol is as popular as it ever was, its brand name virtually synonymous with all other nonaspirin pain relievers of its type.

Johnson & Johnson has continued its strategy of expanding its customer base with new products well into the 1990s by introducing daily-wear disposable contact lenses to the market, and with its purchase of Neutrogena Company, a new line of soaps and skin creams.

Johnson & Johnson is an ever-changing company with a remarkable ability to adapt to the monumental—and virtually daily—changes in worldwide health care needs. With manufacturing subsidiaries in forty-four countries, its marketplace is truly global. Annual revenues are $22.6 billion, with Johnson & Johnson consumer products accounting for 34 percent of these revenues; professional products, 34 percent; and pharmaceuticals, 32 percent.

J.P. Morgan & Co. Inc. (JPM)

J.P. Morgan is an old-line banking and investment firm that specializes in arranging large-scale financing for governments, wealthy individuals, and corporations. Its primary subsidiary is Morgan Guaranty Trust, a major dealer in currencies, derivatives, and government securities.

The company was founded by Junius S. Morgan, who began

his career as partner to London banker George Peabody. Morgan took over the British banking firm when Peabody retired in the early 1860s, changing its name to J.S. Morgan & Co. His New York–based son, Junius Pierpont Morgan, or J.P. for short, began his own financial services company in 1862, and the two firms linked up to become major players in the intercontinental money game as they channeled investment capital from one capital to another back and forth across the Atlantic. Upon Junius S.'s death in 1890, J. Pierpont took over both businesses and reorganized them under the J.P. Morgan & Co. banner.

By 1907, J. Pierpont Morgan—the personification of American capitalism, whose name, in abbreviated form or long, has become virtually synonymous with Wall Street wealth and power—was wielding greater and greater influence. His company had in large part refinanced and restructured the U.S. railroad industry and created the deals that brought U.S. Steel, General Electric, and International Harvester into being. When he died in 1913, his son, J.P. Morgan Jr., assumed leadership of the company in partnership with Thomas Lamont, who ran the firm's daily activities.

The Glass-Steagall Act of 1933 forced the financial behemoth to divide these activities, however. As a result of the company's ensuing reorganization, Morgan stayed in commercial banking and created Morgan Stanley to underwrite securities. In 1959, the Morgan bank merged with the Guaranty Trust Co. to become a holding company, Morgan Guaranty.

During the tumultuous 1960s, Morgan was the country's busiest trader in government securities, and following another restructuring in the 1980s, moved vehemently into the exploding field of mergers and acquisitions.

Since the 1980s, J.P. Morgan has expanded its traditional base of credit and investment management to include swaps and options, and more aggressive kinds of risk management here and abroad, where it quickly extended its financial reach into Eastern Europe following the collapse of the Soviet Union. Some of its global ven-

J.P. MORGAN & COMPANY INC.

nyse
JPM

Commercial & Wholesale Banking, New York.

Funded Dt$22,989,000,000
Shares Pref'd 2,650,000
Shares Com'n 176,457,000

Options
PHILA

Split 2 for 1

Split 2 for 1

SCALE: Ea.
block = $4

YEAR	1983	1984	1985	1986	1987	1988	1989	1990	1991	1992	1993	1994	1995	1996	1997	1998	1999	2000	2001	2002
EARN	2.63	3.04	3.90	4.74	.39	5.38	d7.04	3.99	5.63	5.66	8.48	6.02	6.42	7.63	7.17					
DIV	.93	1.00	1.10	1.23	1.36	1.50	1.66	1.82	1.98	2.18	2.40	2.72	3.00	3.24	3.52					

tures have been winners; others have not, such as Morgan's investment in the Banco de Espanol de Credito (Banesto), which was taken over by the Spanish government when the bank failed. Nevertheless, Morgan has continued to broaden and diversify its activities in the international arena well into the 1990s, particularly in the emerging markets of the Pacific Rim and Latin America.

Annual revenues, which are derived from interest (63 percent), trading (17 percent), corporate financing (4 percent), fees (10 percent) and other sources (6 percent), are in excess of $12 billion. It has more than $130 billion in assets, the largest percentage in trading account, cash and equivalents, and net loan assets.

McDonald's Corporation (MCD)

McDonald's operates, licenses, and services the world's largest chain of fast-food chain restaurants, around 23,000 of them in 111 countries worldwide. Seventy percent of the company's restaurants are owned by franchisees, 19 percent by the company, and the rest by affiliates.

McDonald's is also a real estate company, owning some 60 percent of its locations and long-term leases on virtually all the others. Real estate and restaurant decisions are kept separate financially. Big Mac's annual revenues of more than $33 billion account for approximately 18 percent of fast-food market sales.

While McDonald's has never had an unprofitable year, it ran into some rough spots from 1996 to 1997, when overextension coupled with stiff competition in the fast-food arena slowed domestic sales growth, and the price of its stock declined 22 percent (while the Dow went up 42 percent). Since then, however, with its domestic sales back on track and its foreign markets exploding, it is again one of the best-performing stocks on the Dow, and there seems to be almost no limit to the growth potential of McDonald's (although its stock will probably always be too overpriced for the taste of a Dow Dogs hunter like me).

McDONALD'S CORPORATION

nyse
MCD

SCALE: Ea.
block = $2

Options
CBOE

Fast Food Restaurants: Franchising.

Funded Dt $4,834,000,000
Shares Pref'd . . . None
Shares Com'n 685,853,000

The stock of this co. is included
in the DOW-JONES INDUST'L AVERAGE.

Split 3 for 2
Split 3 for 2
Split 3 for 2
Split 3 for 2
Split 2 for 1
Split 2 for 1

80
70
60
50
40
30
20
10

YEAR	1981	1982	1983	1984	1985	1986	1987	1988	1989	1990	1991	1992	1993	1994	1995	1996	1997	1998	1999	2000
EARN	.33	.37	.43	.49	.56	.62	.72	.86	.98	1.10	1.18	1.30	1.45	1.68	1.97	2.21	2.29			
DIV	.05	.06	.08	.09	.10	.11	.13	.14	.16	.17	.18	.20	.21	.23	.26	.29	.32			

Merck & Co. Inc. (MRK)

Merck is the premier prescription pharmaceutical company in the world, with a total market share of almost 5 percent.

Unlike many pharmaceutical companies, Merck has emphasized massive investment in basic research, averaging between $500 million and $700 million annually in recent years. The result has been such widely used products as Aldomet and Vasotec (hypertensives), Meloxin and Primaxin (antibiotics), Timopic (for glaucoma), Mevacor (for lowering cholesterol), Pepcid (for ulcers and acid reflux), and Clinoril and Indocin (anti-inflammatory medicines).

The Human and Animal Health Products sector, which contributes more than 90 percent of the company's $23.6 billion annual sales, produces drugs that are important in treating livestock. Its Heartgard-30 for the prevention of heartworm in dogs is the leading pharmaceutical product for small animals.

Merck also has a Specialty Chemicals Division, which includes Calgon Corporation, known best for water purification but which also produces wound dressings; and Kelco Division, which makes alginates and xanthan gum used in processed foods, oil field applications, and other industrial and consumer products. Merck has also entered into profitable joint ventures with Dow 30 compatriots Johnson & Johnson and du Pont.

Not surprisingly, this darling of institutional portfolios is no bargain at the moment. What is?

Minnesota Mining and Manufacturing Company (MMM)

This remarkable organization has been built on a steady stream of new products, some 60,000 in all, that are largely the inventions of some 86,000 employees in 322 offices in fifty countries, including the United States. Scotch tape and Post-it flags (which were invented by a 3M scientist who sang in a church choir and got frustrated every time the page marker fell out of his hymnal) are the most familiar examples.

MERCK & COMPANY INC.

nyse
MRK

Ethical Drugs/Specialty Chemicals.

Options
ASE, CBOE

Funded Dt $1,845,000,000
Shares Pref'd . . . None
Shs Com'n 1,195,259,000

The Stock of this company is included
in the DOW-JONES INDUSTRIAL AVERAGE.

Split 2 for 1
Split 3 for 1
Split 3 for 1

SCALE: Ea.
block = $4

YEAR	1983	1984	1985	1986	1987	1988	1989	1990	1991	1992	1993	1994	1995	1996	1997	1998	1999	2000	2001	2002
EARN	.34	.37	.42	.54	.74	1.02	1.26	1.52	1.83	2.12	1.87	2.38	2.44	3.12	3.74					
DIV	.16	.17	.18	.21	.27	.43	.55	.64	.77	.92	1.03	1.14	1.24	1.42	1.69					

160
140
120
100
80
60
40
20

MINNESOTA MINING & MANUFACTURING COMPANY

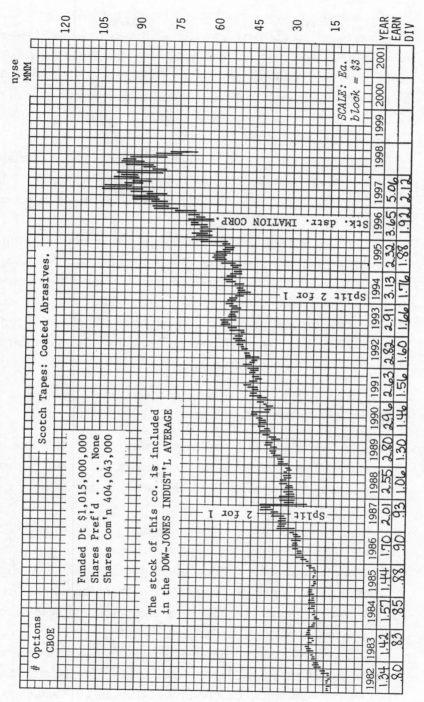

nyse
MMM

Scotch Tapes: Coated Abrasives.

Options
CBOE

Funded Dt $1,015,000,000
Shares Pref'd . . . None
Shares Com'n 404,043,000

The stock of this co. is included
in the DOW-JONES INDUST'L AVERAGE

SCALE: Ea.
block = $3

Stk. dstr. IMATION CORP.

Split 2 for 1

2 for 1 Split

YEAR	1982	1983	1984	1985	1986	1987	1988	1989	1990	1991	1992	1993	1994	1995	1996	1997	1998	1999	2000	2001
EARN	1.34	1.42	1.57	1.44	1.70	2.01	2.55	2.80	2.94	2.63	2.82	2.91	3.13	2.32	3.65	5.06				
DIV	.80	.83	.85	.88	.90	.93	1.06	1.30	1.46	1.56	1.60	1.66	1.76	1.88	1.92	2.12				

3M coats adhesives to film (Scotch brand tapes), abrasive granulates to paper (sandpaper), low-tack adhesives to paper (Post-it brand notes), iron oxide to plastic backing (magnetic recording tape), glass beads to plastic backing (reflective sign materials), light-sensitive materials to metal (printing plates), nutrients to film (bacteria culture dishes), ceramics to granules (roofing granules), and dozens of others.

But coatings are just one product category. Others include nonwoven fibers, fluorochemistry, industrial abrasives, and hardware ranging from hand-held tape dispensers to sophisticated equipment for open-heart surgery.

A large percentage of 3M's $15 billion annual revenues come from abroad, and this percentage of international sales is increasing, which makes 3M more susceptible than many companies to currency fluctuations. About 50 percent of sales are to service-related businesses, 40 percent to industry, and 10 percent to consumers. Thirty percent of sales come from new products introduced in the past fifteen years.

Philip Morris Companies Inc. (MO)

Philip Morris, an old-line-tobacco firm, is not only the most successful and profitable tobacco company in the world, but the largest and most diversified food and beverage company in the United States.

The company's diversification began in 1970 with Miller Brewing Company, which had a big success with the introduction of Lite beer. During the 1980s, though, its flagship Miller High Life lost significant market share to competitors. Its newest beer, Miller Genuine Draft, is the fastest-growing premium beer on the market, accounting for 10 percent of MO's sales.

Philip Morris acquired Seven-Up in 1978, and following an unsuccessful effort to market a caffeine-free lemon-lime drink called Like, it sold Seven-Up's domestic operations in 1986.

PHILIP MORRIS COMPANIES INC.

nyse
MO

SCALE: Ea. block = $2

Options
ASE

Holding Company: Largest Tobacco Co. In World, Largest U.S. Food Processor, Brewery "MILLER HIGH LIFE", etc.

F'd Debt $15,462,000,000
Shares Pref'd . . . None
Shares Com 2,427,926,000

The stock of this company is included in the DOW-JONES INDUSTRIAL AVERAGE.

Split 2 for 1

Split 4 for 1

Split 3 for 1

YEAR	1982	1983	1984	1985	1986	1987	1988	1989	1990	1991	1992	1993	1994	1995	1996	1997	1998	1999	2000	2001
EARN	.26	.30	.30	.44	.52	.65	.74	1.06	1.28	1.41	1.82	1.35	1.82	2.17	2.56					
DIV	.10	.12	.14	.16	.19	.25	.32	.39	.49	.61	.74	.87	.95	1.16	1.40	1.60				

The $5.7 billion purchase of General Foods in 1986 brought such well-known products as Maxwell House coffee, Jell-O, Birds Eye frozen foods, and Oscar Meyer into the fold. The $13-billion acquisition in 1988 of Kraft Inc., with Kraft cheeses, Breyers ice cream, Parkay margarine, Light n' Lively, and a range of popular food brands, gave the combined Kraft General Food Division 10 percent of the U.S. brand-food market.

Philip Morris is one of the richest and best-managed companies in the world. But long run (and perhaps even short run), tobacco revenues, which today account for almost 60 percent of the company's approximately $70-plus billion annual sales, have a poor projection given the current atmosphere of antitobacco rhetoric and legislation that hangs over the industry like an angry black cloud of secondhand smoke.

Procter & Gamble Company (PG)

Procter & Gamble's identification with such household staples as Ivory soap, Mr. Clean, Head & Shoulders, Crest toothpaste, Pampers, Charmin, Bounty, and Tide has made it one of the most visible consumer products companies in the world. Although personal care and household products amount to some 80 percent of the company's approximately $30.1 billion annual sales, Procter & Gamble's food products are equally familiar: Folgers coffee, Crisco, Pringles potato chips, and Duncan Hines cake mixes.

Its acquisitions have included the German toothpaste company Blandex, and the proprietary drug companies Richardson Vicks Inc. and G.D. Searles. Nearly 40 percent of sales come from its expanding international activities.

Procter & Gamble is one of the world's great companies. It has superb domestic and international marketing and a diverse product base not really vulnerable to economic cycles. It is active in research and development, especially in the potentially exploding area of pharmaceuticals, and is a financially rock-solid firm that

PROCTER & GAMBLE COMPANY

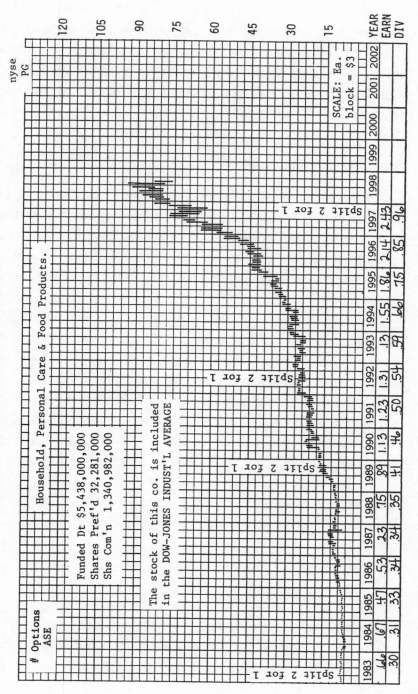

Household, Personal Care & Food Products.

nyse
PG

Funded Dt $5,438,000,000
Shares Pref'd 32,281,000
Shs Com'n 1,340,982,000

The stock of this co. is included
in the DOW-JONES INDUST'L AVERAGE

Options
ASE

SCALE: Ea.
block = $3

Split 2 for 1

	1983	1984	1985	1986	1987	1988	1989	1990	1991	1992	1993	1994	1995	1996	1997	1998	1999	2000	2001	2002
YEAR																				
EARN	.66	.67	.47	.53	.23	.75	.89	1.13	1.23	1.31	.12	1.55	1.86	2.14	2.43					
DIV	.30	.31	.33	.34	.34	.35	.41	.46	.50	.54	.59	.66	.75	.85	.96					

will probably continue its steady and profitable growth in the next century. But one thing about companies this good is that there's not much excitement on the upside, and should something happen to the downside, there's plenty of room to drop, especially in today's extravagantly overpriced market. Needless to say, that's when I—and you—should get interested.

Sears, Roebuck & Company (S)

Sears started as a mail-order operation, specializing in just about everything except brides. When the automobile brought everything in America within closer reach, Sears began opening retail stores, eventually becoming America's largest retailer. In 1972, Sears' sales amounted to 1 percent of the United States gross national product.

But Sears is also a financial services giant. It acquired Allstate Insurance, a provider of property and liability, back in 1921. It has been a Dow stock since 1924, and it was the first to diversify into unrelated financial services.

In the 1980s, Sears acquired Dean Witter Financial Services, engaged in brokerage, investment banking, consumer finance, and mortgage banking; Coldwell Banker, a developer, manager, and broker of real estate; and introduced the Discover credit card.

Its annual revenues of around $50.1 billion typically break down as follows: merchandising, 37 percent; property and liability insurance, 38 percent; life insurance, 8 percent; financial services and the rest, 17 percent.

Travelers Group Inc. (TRV)

The Travelers has replaced Primerica on the Dow literally in name only—because it is Primerica, but under a different umbrella (pun intended).

One of the largest insurance providers in the United States, the

SEARS, ROEBUCK & COMPANY

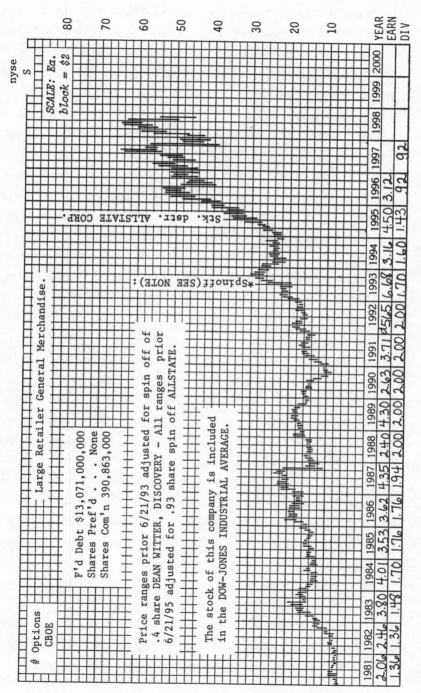

nyse
S

SCALE: Ea.
block = $2

Options
CBOE

——— Large Retailer General Merchandise.

F'd Debt $13,071,000,000
Shares Pref'd . . . None
Shares Com'n 390,863,000

Price ranges prior 6/21/93 adjusted for spin off of
.4 share DEAN WITTER, DISCOVERY — All ranges prior
6/21/95 adjusted for .93 share spin off ALLSTATE.

The stock of this company is included
in the DOW-JONES INDUSTRIAL AVERAGE.

Stk. distr. ALLSTATE CORP.

*Spinoff (SEE NOTE):

	1981	1982	1983	1984	1985	1986	1987	1988	1989	1990	1991	1992	1993	1994	1995	1996	1997	1998	1999	2000	YEAR
	2.06	2.46	3.80	4.01	3.53	3.62	4.35	2.40	4.30	2.63	3.71	4.565	6.68	3.16	4.50	3.12	.92				EARN
	1.36	1.36	1.48	1.70	1.76	1.76	1.94	2.00	2.00	2.00	2.00	2.00	1.70	1.60	1.43						DIV

Travelers entered the 1990s looking to expand its financial services activities, but some bad investments made in the 1980s came home to roost and the company fell vulnerable to a takeover.

Sanford "Sandy" Weill's Primerica, the financial services conglomerate whose activities ranged from brokerage services, consumer financing, credit cards, and mutual funds to insurance, was looking to add such profitable adjuncts as life and property casualty insurance services, and gobbled the Travelers up. Weill spun off the Travelers' health care operations and dumped the Primerica moniker, retaining the insurance giant's more familiar name and easily identifiable red umbrella logo for the new company's all-inclusive operations.

Founded by James Batterson and some other Hartford, Connecticut, businessmen in 1864, the Travelers began life as an accident insurance company, diversifying into life insurance annuities and liability insurance during the latter half of the nineteenth century.

By shrewdly investing in U.S. government bonds rather than stocks, the company successfully weathered the Great Crash, and grew by leaps and bounds during World War II as an insurer of government projects. It branched out into mutual fund services with its 1979 purchase of Keystone, and into investment banking with its buyout of Dillon, Read in 1986. During the high-rolling '80s, it also began sinking a lot of its profits into real estate. But when that market took a nosedive in the late '80s to early '90s, the company, scrambling hard to recoup heavy losses, began selling off many of its underperforming businesses and laying off thousands of workers.

The acquisitive Weill spotted an opportunity, Primerica opened its jaws, and the rest is Wall Street history.

Primerica began life in 1901 as American Can Company. Over time, the company diversified into such disparate activities as paper and forest products, record stores, and catalog sales.

It began dabbling in life insurance in 1981 with its takeover of

Associated Madison. In 1986, the canning operation was sold (the record store division had already been jettisoned), and the company's emphasis shifted to financial services. Renamed Primerica in 1987, the company was purchased by Weill's Commercial Credit Corporation a year later.

Weill sold off the paper and forest products and catalog sales components to focus the company's energies exclusively on its core insurance and financial businesses; he capped off this strategy with the $4-billion buyout of the Travelers in 1993. In addition to its Travelers subsidiaries, the company's holdings include Smith Barney Shearson Inc.

Under the Travelers Group Inc. umbrella, sales have averaged around $7 billion annually since the 1993 buyout that eventually saw Primerica disappear from the Dow—but, as I've said, in name only.

TRAVELERS GROUP INC.

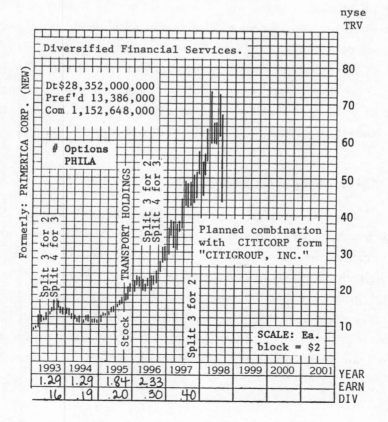

Union Carbide Corporation (UK)

For sixty-odd years, through the 1970s, Union Carbide was a solid producer of chemicals, ranking second only to du Pont. Then came the recession of the early 1980s, which pounded this cyclical industry in general and Union Carbide in particular.

Using cost advantages from its strength in basic chemicals, it gained significant market share in such consumer products as antifreeze, batteries, and plastic wrappings like Glad Bags.

Then came the infamous 1984 deadly gas leak in Bhopal, India, that claimed the lives of more than three thousand people. The case was finally settled in 1989. The Bhopal disaster was followed a year later by a hostile takeover attempt led by Samuel Heyman, head of GAF Corporation.

To fend off the takeover, Carbide sold its consumer products division, its agricultural division, and its Connecticut headquarters for $3.5 billion, and paid shareholders $4.5 billion in special dividends and other payments. It preserved its independence, but at great cost—a heavy debt burden that saw the quality rating of its bonds plummet, and the loss of its most promising activities.

Union Carbide in the 1990s has been back to basics, a cyclical business sitting in a down cycle. But the company has made significant reductions in its debt and regained the investment-grade credit rating it lost in 1985. Annual revenues are $6.5 billion.

United Technologies Corporation (UTX)

United Technologies has sales of $24.7 billion from three categories. Aerospace and defense, providing about 48 percent of the company's revenues, comprises Pratt & Whitney jet engines and Flight Systems (Sikorski helicopters, Hamilton Standard, Missiles and Space Systems). Commercial and Industrial, providing 46 percent, comprises Building Systems (Otis elevators and Carrier HVC heating, ventilating, and air-conditioning equipment). Industrial Systems (electronic, electromechanical, hydraulic systems and

UNION CARBIDE CORPORATION

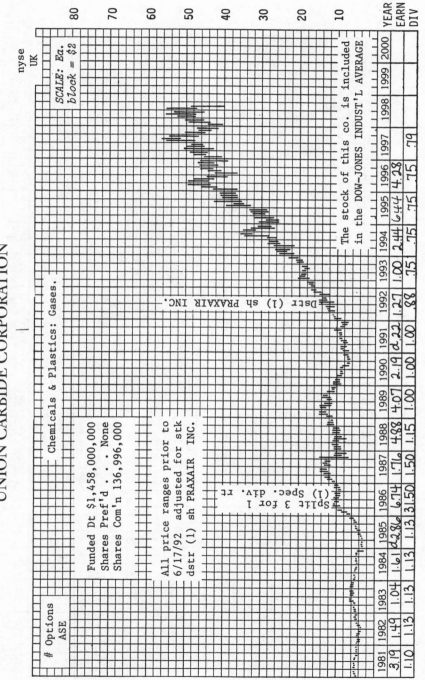

Options
ASE

Chemicals & Plastics: Gases.

SCALE: Ea.
block = $2

Funded Dt $1,458,000,000
Shares Pref'd . . . None
Shares Com'n 136,996,000

All price ranges prior to
6/17/92 adjusted for stk
dstr (1) sh PRAXAIR INC.

Dstr (1) sh PRAXAIR INC.

Split 3 for 1
(1) Spec. div. rt

The stock of this co. is included
in the DOW-JONES INDUST'L AVERAGE

YEAR	1981	1982	1983	1984	1985	1986	1987	1988	1989	1990	1991	1992	1993	1994	1995	1996	1997	1998	1999	2000
EARN	3.19	1.49	1.04	1.61	d2.28	6.74	1.76	4.88	4.07	2.19	d2.22	1.27	1.00	2.44	6.44	4.28				
DIV	1.10	1.13	1.13	1.13	1.13	31.50	1.50	1.15	1.00	1.00	1.00	.88	.75	.75	.75	.75	.79			

UNITED TECHNOLOGIES CORPORATION

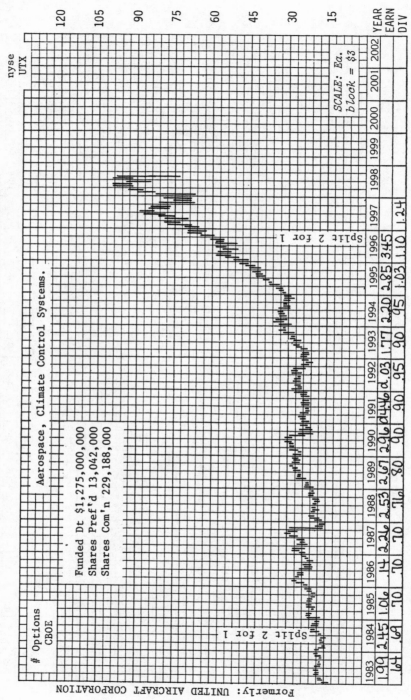

nyse
UTX

Aerospace, Climate Control Systems.

Funded Dt $1,275,000,000
Shares Pref'd 13,042,000
Shares Com'n 229,188,000

Options CBOE

SCALE: Ea.
block = $3

Formerly: UNITED AIRCRAFT CORPORATION

Split 2 for 1

Split 2 for 1

YEAR	1983	1984	1985	1986	1987	1988	1989	1990	1991	1992	1993	1994	1995	1996	1997	1998	1999	2000	2001	2002
EARN	1.99	2.45	1.06	.14	2.22	2.53	2.67	2.96	a.44	a.03	1.77	2.20	2.85	3.45						
DIV	.64	.69	.70	.70	.70	.76	.80	.90	.90	.95	.90	.95	1.03	1.10	1.24					

components for the automotive industry) represents 6 percent.

Although military and space-related work represents less than 25 percent of revenues, the company remains vulnerable to reduced government spending in these areas. Otis has 24 percent of the global new-equipment market, twice the market share of its nearest competitor. Service and modernization account for half its revenue, so it is only partly hostage to the commercial construction industry.

Carrier is also the world's market share leader and has particular strength in Europe and the Far East, with the exception of Japan, where despite that country's economic woes, local competition remains formidable and where Carrier is trying to improve its competitive position.

UT Automotive supplies the Big Three automakers in various ways (electrical systems, door trim, keyless entry systems, and the like), and its wire systems and engine-cooling business enjoys growing demand in the European auto market. It owns Sheller-Globe Corporation, a leading supplier of steering wheels, instrument panels, and other automotive components.

United Technologies has a lot of potential, especially in the jet engine market, but its heavy involvement with the recession-sensitive automotive and construction industries may always make things somewhat iffy.

Wal-Mart Stores Inc. (WMT)

Sam Walton is Arkansas' second most famous favorite son after President Bill Clinton, and probably its most financially successful. The chain of Wal-Mart discount department stores, and cash-and-carry membership-only Sam's Wholesale Clubs he lent his name to, boasts 2,836 outlets in the United States.

The largest and most rapidly growing retailer on the North American continent, Wal-Mart has taken full advantage of the North American Free Trade Agreement (NAFTA) passed by

Congress and signed by President Clinton, and opened stores in Canada and Mexico, as well as the United States.

Patterning his operation on the five-and-dime concept of offering quality merchandise at low-as-they'll-go prices, Sam Walton opened his first Wal-Mart in 1962. By 1970, he'd opened eighteen stores in America with combined sales of $44 million annually, and the company went public. In an effort to sustain the company's image as *the* bargain retailer while continuing to expand rapidly, Wal-Mart put a number of systems in place, such as a highly automated distribution center (for reducing shipping time and costs) and computerized inventory procedures (to accelerate checkout and reordering) that have been routinely adopted by most other retailers today. By 1982, sales had grown to $1.2 billion from 276 stores.

A year later, the first Sam's Wholesale Club was opened. It offered consumers who paid an annual fee of about $25 even deeper discounts on many of the items sold at Wal-Mart, but stocked here in larger, commercial-sized quantities. The number of Sam's Clubs has today grown to almost five hundred outlets, though this growth has slowed somewhat in recent years due to increased competition from similar wholesale warehouse stores that have sprung up around the country.

In the late 1970s, Wal-Mart entered the acquisition game, which it continued playing throughout the 1980s and into the 1990s by adding to its holdings Mohr Value, Hutchinson Wholesale Shoes, Big-K Department Stores, Super-Saver Warehouse Clubs, and distribution services firm McLane Company.

In 1987, Wal-Mart joined forces with a Dallas, Texas, supermarket chain, Cullum Companies, to combine the discount retail store and supermarket concepts into a giant crossbreed with a mall-like atmosphere called Hypermart*USA; it offered consumers 200,000 square feet of floor space in which they could shop until they dropped.

In 1994, Wal-Mart bought up more than 120 Woolco stores

WAL-MART STORES INC.

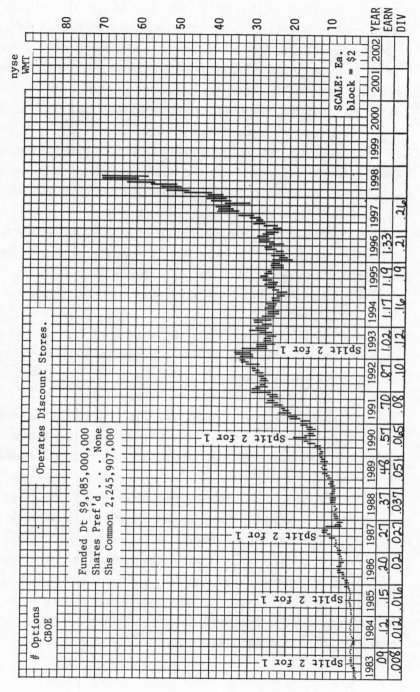

nyse
WMT

Operates Discount Stores.

Funded Dt $9,085,000,000
Shares Pref'd . . . None
Shs Common 2,245,907,000

Options
CBOE

SCALE: Ea.
block = $2

Split 2 for 1 (1983)
Split 2 for 1 (1985)
Split 2 for 1 (1987)
Split 2 for 1 (1990)
Split 2 for 1 (1993)

	1983	1984	1985	1986	1987	1988	1989	1990	1991	1992	1993	1994	1995	1996	1997	1998	1999	2000	2001	2002	YEAR
EARN	.09	.12	.15	.20	.27	.37	.48	.57	.70	.87	1.02	1.17	1.19	1.33							
DIV	.008	.012	.016	.02	.027	.037	.051	.065	.08	.10	.12	.16	.19	.21	.26						

from Woolworth's as that elder statesman of American retailers began showing signs of slippage, and converted them to Wal-Mart stores, expanding the Wal-Mart landscape in the company's biggest single jump up to that time. Sam Walton never got to see it, however. He died in 1992, and with his passing, some say, went much of the personal touch he sought to bring to the retailing giant as a way of separating it from the competition.

Walton would regularly visit his thousands of stores and get to know employees by name so they would pass along to their customers the same sense of friendliness and caring he communicated to them, and keep those customers coming back.

After Sam Walton's passing, the chain was also hit by controversy when its patriotic "Buy American" sloganeering boomeranged; investigative reporters spilled the beans that a considerable amount of Wal-Mart's merchandise was actually made abroad, much of it in Mexico and China.

Some towns have also blocked the opening of Wal-Mart stores in their localities for competitive reasons, perceiving the company's aggressive discounting methods and sense of Manifest Destiny to be examples of "capitalistic greed" run rampant.

Other localities have denied Wal-Mart access on aesthetic grounds because of the chain's resistance to adapt the distinctive "everywhere-the-same" look of its stores to the architectural desires of these communities.

However, in spite of these occasional setbacks to its image as the giant superstore with the personal ("Welcome to Wal-Mart") mom-and-pop-store touch, annual revenues are $117.9 billion. About half of sales come from soft goods (apparel) and hard goods (hardware, housewares, auto supplies, and small appliances). The remaining half come from stationery and candy; sporting goods and toys; gifts, CDs, tapes, and electronics; health and beauty aids; pharmaceuticals; jewelry; and shoes.

The Walt Disney Company (DIS)

This fantasy empire hinged its fortunes on turning the squeak of a mouse into the roar of a lion king. A giant entertainment conglomerate, it is involved not only in film, television, and music production, but theme parks, book publishing, Broadway theater, retail merchandise stores, and a host of other ancillary activities.

The company was started by illustrator Walt Disney and his businessman brother Roy, who entered the motion picture industry during the halcyon days of the early silent cinema, building their own studio in 1923. Specializing in animated short subjects—a field, unlike live action, with few competitors at the time—Walt introduced his immortal screen creation Mickey Mouse to audiences in *Plane Crazy*, a silent cartoon released in 1928, a year after the talkies were born. In 1929, he gave Mickey a voice in *Steamboat Willie*, the first talkie cartoon. Walt provided the voice for Mickey himself in the Oscar-winning groundbreaker, and continued to do so in every Mickey Mouse film thereafter, until his death (Walt's that is, not Mickey's) in 1966.

Their short films a success, Walt and Roy expanded horizons by moving into full-length animated features with such classics as *Snow White and the Seven Dwarfs* (1937), and *Fantasia* and *Pinocchio* (both 1940). *The Mickey Mouse Club* and *The Wonderful World of Disney* were launched on the relatively new medium of television in 1955, the latter show running, on and off, for twenty-nine years, first with Walt as host, and most recently with Disney COO Michael Eisner handling the job. It is primarily Eisner who has spearheaded and presided over the greatest era of creativity, innovation, and prosperity in Disney Company history.

With the opening of Disneyland in Anaheim, California, in 1955, the Disney organization entered the theme park business in an attempt to bring its visual fantasies to life. It was a roaring success, and a larger version of it, called Disneyworld, opened in Orlando, Florida, in 1971. The company enlarged its sunbelt empire with Epcot Center in 1982, the Disney-MGM Studios in 1989, and Animal Kingdom in 1998.

Convinced by the enormous influx of overseas tourists to its Florida theme parks that the world would enjoy homegrown versions of the Disney experience, the company opened Tokyo Disneyland in 1984; it was followed by Euro Disney, built outside Paris, in 1992. The controversial Euro Disney, however, which the French initially resisted on the grounds of "cultural corruption," has not matched the success of the company's American and Japanese counterparts, having lost more than $500 million since it opened. A proposed theme park dealing with American history to be built near a Civil War battlefield in Virginia met with controversy, too. Local residents resisted having their hallowed ground Disneyfied, and the idea was scrapped.

Disney has continued to dominate the animated feature film with such blockbusters as *Beauty and the Beast* (1991) and *The Lion King* (1994), both of which were turned by Disney into hit Broadway musicals. The company also derives considerable income from the Disney Channel cable-TV network; Touchstone Pictures, its live action, more adult-oriented feature film wing; Miramax Films, America's leading distributor of independently made movies geared toward audiences with a thirst for more than mainstream Hollywood fare; Hollywood Records; and 265 Disney stores selling Disney merchandise and memorabilia worldwide.

Disney's film, TV, and recording activities account for 43 percent of the company's $5.5 billion revenues; its theme parks, 40 percent; and the rest, 17 percent. As there will always be a need for entertainment, there will always be a Disney, so I don't expect this stock will ever be truly "cheap." But who knows? Stranger things have happened, like turning the squeak of a mouse into the roar of a lion.

THE WALT DISNEY COMPANY

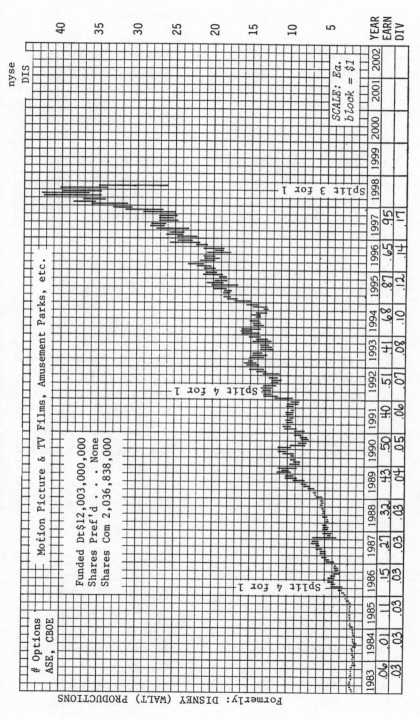

Formerly: DISNEY (WALT) PRODUCTIONS

nyse
DIS

Options
ASE, CBOE

Motion Picture & TV Films, Amusement Parks, etc.

Funded Dt$12,003,000,000
Shares Pref'd . . . None
Shares Com 2,036,838,000

SCALE: Ea.
block = $1

Split 3 for 1

Split 4 for 1

Split 4 for 1

YEAR	1983	1984	1985	1986	1987	1988	1989	1990	1991	1992	1993	1994	1995	1996	1997	1998	1999	2000	2001	2002
EARN	.06	.01	.11	.15	.21	.32	.43	.50	.40	.51	.41	.68	.87	.65	.95					
DIV	.03	.03	.03	.03	.03	.03	.04	.05	.06	.07	.08	.10	.12	.14	.17					

The Dow Companies' Offices

AlliedSignal Inc.
Columbia Road
Morristown, NJ 07962-2497
201-455-2000

Aluminum Company of America
425 6th Avenue
Pittsburgh, PA 15219-1850
412-553-4545

American Express Company
American Express Tower
World Financial Center
New York, NY 10285
212-640-2000

AT&T Corporation
32 Avenue of the Americas
New York, NY 10013-5400
212-387-5400

The Boeing Company
7755 East Marginal Way South
Seattle, WA 98108
206-655-2121

Caterpillar Inc.
100 NE Adams Street
Peoria, IL 61629
309-675-1000

Chevron Corporation
225 Bush Avenue
San Francisco, CA 91404
415-894-7700

The Coca-Cola Company
1 Coca-Cola Plaza
Atlanta, GA 30313
404-676-2121

E.I. du Pont de Nemours and Company
1007 Market Street
Wilmington, DE 19898
302-774-1000

Eastman Kodak Company
343 State Street
Rochester, NY 14650
716-724-4000

Exxon Corporation
225 John W. Carpenter Freeway
Irving, TX 75602-2298
214-444-1000

General Electric Company
3135 Easton Turnpike
Fairfield, CT 06431-0001
203-373-2459

General Motors Corporation
3044 West Grand Boulevard
Detroit, MI 48202-3091
313-556-5000

Goodyear Tire & Rubber Company
1144 East Market Street
Akron, OH 44316-0001
314-796-2121

Hewlett-Packard
3000 Hanover Street
Palo Alto, CA 94304
415-857-1501

International Paper Company
2 Manhattanville Road
Purchase, NY 10577
914-397-1596

J.P. Morgan & Co. Inc.
60 Wall Street
New York, NY 10260-0060
212-483-2323

Merck & Co. Inc.
P.O. Box 1000
Whitehouse Station, NJ 08889-1000
908-594-4662

Philip Morris Companies
120 Park Avenue
New York, NY 10017
212-880-5000

Sears, Roebuck & Company
Sears Tower
Chicago, IL 60684
312-875-2500

Union Carbide Corporation
39 Old Ridgebury Road
Danbury, CT 06817
203-794-2000

**International Business
Machines Corporation**
Old Orchard Road
Armonk, NY 10504
416-765-1900

Johnson & Johnson
One Johnson & Johnson
   Plaza
New Brunswick, NJ 08933
908-524-0400

McDonald's Corporation
McDonald's Plaza
Oak Brook, IL 60521
708-575-3000

**Minnesota Mining and
Manufacturing Company**
3M Center Building
St. Paul, MN 55144-1000
612-733-1110

Procter & Gamble Company
1 Procter & Gamble Plaza
Cincinnati, OH 45202
513-983-1100

The Travelers Group, Inc.
65 E. 55th Street
New York, NY 10022
212-891-8900

**United Technologies
Corporation**
United Technologies
   Building
Hartford, CT 06101
203-728-7000

Wal-Mart Stores, Inc.	The Walt Disney
Bentonville, AR 72716	Company
501-273-4000	500 S. Buena Vista Street
	Burbank, CA 91521
	818-560-1000

My Beating the Dow Basic Five-Stock Method

My stock-picking system for beating the Dow is predicated upon the idea that the out-of-favor, or "worst"-performing, companies on the Dow (my pet Dow Dogs) do a lot better over time than the top, or "best"—performing, ones.

My Five-Stock formula is the simplest way of outperforming the Dow with that strategy. It uses a combination of the highest-yielding and least-expensive stocks to structure a five-stock portfolio; this has the incidental advantage of requiring less capital because of fewer stocks and lower prices. (For more advanced stock-picking methods, the reader is again referred to my first book.)

This basic method has produced super returns; I'll give you the actual statistics a bit later. You can get these returns because my Beating the Dow Five-Stock Strategy offers you two big advantages over the pros. One is the freedom to operate in a universe as small as the Dow stocks. The other is the freedom to buy and sell according to *your* timetable, not one that is dictated by your clients or someone else.

Seven Simple Steps to Super Returns

Follow these seven easy steps to achieving extraordinary returns:

Step 1: Prepare a Stock Planning Worksheet

Clip out Figure 11.1 and use as is. Or buy a pad of accounting paper and reproduce your own version by listing the Dow stocks alphabetically, as pictured, next to their symbols in the left-hand columns

	Symbol	Dow Stock	Closing Price	Yield	Rank	Lowest Rank	Execution Price	Closing Price End	Dividends	Total Return
1	ALD	AlliedSignal								
2	AA	Aluminum Co. of America								
3	AXP	American Express								
4	T	American Tel. & Tel.								
5	BA	Boeing								
6	CAT	Caterpillar								
7	CHV	Chevron								
8	KO	Coca-Cola								
9	DD	Dupont								
10	EK	Eastman Kodak								
11	XON	Exxon								
12	GE	General Electric								
13	GM	General Motors								
14	GT	Goodyear Tire & Rubber								
15	HWP	Hewlett-Packard								
16	IBM	Int'l Business Machines								
17	IP	International Paper								
18	JNJ	Johnson & Johnson								
19	MCD	McDonald's								
20	MRK	Merck								
21	MMM	Minnesota Mining & Mfg.								
22	JPM	JP Morgan								
23	MO	Philip Morris								
24	PG	Procter & Gamble								
25	S	Sears, Roebuck								
26	TRV	Travelers Group								
27	UK	Union Carbide								
28	UTX	United Technologies								
29	WMT	Wal-Mart Stores								
30	DIS	Walt Disney								

Figure 11.1. Stock Planning Worksheet.

numbered 1 and 2. The symbols will help you make sure you're looking at the right stock when you turn to the newspaper stock tables.

Following the same form used in Figure 11.1, label column 3
"closing prices," column 4 "yield," column 5 "rank," column 6
"lowest prices," and column 7 "execution price."

Step 2: List the Closing Prices

Open up *Barron's* again since you've already got it handy, or get the
Wall Street Journal, the *New York Times*, or any other paper with a
comprehensive business and financial section. Turn to the New
York Stock Exchange Composite listings, the basic stock tables for-
mat you learned how to read in Chapter 4. All the Dow industrials
are listed on the New York Stock Exchange.

With a highlighter, underline or circle each of the Dow stocks
(using the stock symbol to be sure you're not confusing Coca-Cola
Enterprises with Coca-Cola Company, for example) so you can
easily find them for later reference.

Now transfer the closing prices (those in the newspaper column headed "last") to column 3 of your Stock Planning Worksheet
next to the appropriate stock.

These are the prices you will use as the basis for your portfolio
selection of five stocks after you've performed the next several steps.

Step 3: List the Yields

Transfer the numbers in the newspaper column headed "Yld" (for
example, 5.2 for AlliedSignal, 2.1 for Alcoa, etc.) to column 4 of
your Stock Planning Worksheet.

Step 4: Rank the Yields

Now circle the ten highest yields in column 4. If there's a tie, take
the one with the lower closing price. Then, in column 5, rank the
circled stocks from 1 (the highest yield) to 10 (the lowest). You have
now identified and ranked the ten highest yielders in the Dow.

Step 5: Identify the Five Lowest-Priced High Yielders

In column 6, put a checkmark next to the five circled stocks with the lowest closing prices. You have now identified the five stocks combining the highest yield with the lowest price, which will make up your stock portfolio for the next year.

Step 6: Place Your Order

Placing your order is as easy as picking up the phone and dialing your discount broker's 800 number, or punching a few keys on your computer keyboard and going online. Just provide your account number and give instructions to buy the stock. Most brokers will accept payment on purchases by check between the trade date and the "settlement date," which is three days later. Some firms, however, require that sufficient funds be in your account at the time your order is executed. This is particularly true of online brokers, since they charge your account directly. (See "Step 2: Open an Investment Account" in Chapter 10 for more information about this and other aspects of discount brokerage and online trading.)

Buy an equal dollar amount of each of the five stocks. This enhances returns, since lower-priced stocks, which tend to register greater gains, are bought by brokers in greater quantity.

The simplest and easiest way to order stock is to place a market order, in effect instructing your broker to make the transaction at the prevailing market price—the best price the broker can get for you at that time.

You may, however, want to consider placing a limit order. This can protect you against the order's being executed (actually transacted on the floor of the stock exchange) at an unfavorable price (as could happen in a volatile market). But you run the risk that the order will go unexecuted if the market price fails to hit the price specified in your order.

For example, if AlliedSignal, or ALD, turns up in your five

high-yield/lowest-price stock-pick list at a closing price of 34 7/8, but several days have already passed since ALD closed at that price, it may be higher or lower now, and who knows what will happen to it during today's trading session?

There are two things you can do. You can ask your broker for a quote on ALD, and if it's currently still trading at around 35, or at a price that is acceptable to you, you can place a market order and be pretty well assured that in the few minutes it normally takes to execute a Dow stock trade it will be executed at or near that price.

If, however, the price has risen or you have reason to think you'll get a poor execution (for example, the market is going haywire when you call or go online), you can place a limit order instructing your broker to execute the order *only if the price drops to 35 or better*. Limit orders can be placed for a day, a week, a month, or can be placed on a "good till canceled" basis. They can be used on the sell side as well, in which case you tell the broker to execute only if the price rises to the limit price or better.

My feeling is that the degree of protection against volatility afforded by limit orders is not significant enough, and the returns with my Beating the Dow Five-Stock Strategy are significant enough, that the risk of a market order is preferable to the risk of having the order not executed.

You may be tempted to place a *stop-loss* order, but I strongly advise against doing so. A stop-loss order, which becomes a market order to sell when a stock's price declines to a level specified by you, is designed to protect against losses; but you may find yourself selling out a stock that is merely fluctuating, and that will have a net gain for the period over which returns are being measured.

Whatever type of order you place, if you place it by phone, be sure to request that it be read back to you so that there is no misunderstanding. Touch-Tone phone ordering via an 800 number provides this verification automatically, usually by automated voice. With online ordering, of course, you'll see your order up there on your computer screen in glorious black and white—or color. No misunderstanding anything there!

Normally, a broker will confirm the price to you while you're still on the phone or online, or call you back or leave an e-mail message in a matter of minutes. The execution price should be entered in column 7 of your Stock Planning Worksheet. That will be your basis for calculating price changes a year later, so keep this data in a safe place where you know you'll find it 365 days from now!

Step 7: Take Stock and Revamp

A year later, take out your Stock Planning Worksheet, get the newspaper, and list the closing prices at period's end in column 8. The difference between the prices at which the order was originally executed and the closing prices at the end of the period (the selling prices of stocks replaced) plus dividends received during the year equals your total return for each stock.

To get your portfolio return, you add up the totals for each stock and divide the sum by five.

After you've gone through my asset allocation formula in Chapter 10 next January—and if the results once more point to stocks as the asset class of choice—repeat the same process.

Impressive Results

How has my Beating the Dow Five-Stock method performed?

Up to 1991, when I introduced it in my first book, it had produced four times the cumulative return of the Dow Jones Industrial Average over the previous seventeen years (see Table 11.1) with only one losing year (compared to *five* losing years for stocks in general).

Since then, my basic Five-Stock method has worked even better, beating the Dow by 103 percent—a performance almost none of the pros has been able to match.

Table 11.1
Total Return Comparison

Year	5 Lowest Priced	DJIA
1973	28.96%	−13.12%
1974	−3.35%	−23.14%
1975	70.07%	44.40%
1976	48.07%	22.72%
1977	−12.73%	−12.71%
1978	−3.72%	2.69%
1979	13.93%	10.52%
1980	32.84%	21.41%
1981	4.71%	−3.40%
1982	13.20%	25.79%
1983	68.01%	25.65%
1984	−20.00%	1.08%
1985	13.00%	32.78%
1986	−24.70%	26.92%
1987	58.74%	6.02%
1988	23.56%	15.95%
1989	4.57%	31.71%
	1009.75%	**499.35%**

CONCLUSION

Betting The Family Farm on the odds-on favorite may not be the way to win big, but it can be the way to lose big if the favorite doesn't come in.

Stocks today are in that position. They're the odds-on favorite. Because of this, the stock market in general is more extravagantly overpriced than ever before in our history, so it's become tougher to make money on stocks; yet, at the same time, riskier to own them in the event of a major decline.

By the same token, U.S. Government Treasury bonds and Treasury bills are fairly undervalued in relation to their historical levels.

Therefore, with equities so dangerously overvalued and stock prices at such all-time highs, T-bonds and T-bills—considered the ugly stepsiblings of stocks—may, in fact, be the only way to win.

An enhancement to my original stocks-only Beating the Dow strategy, my Beating the Dow with T-bonds, T-bills, and Stocks system consequently includes the use of all three investment sectors, depending upon the relative attractiveness of each sector at the beginning of each year. It gives you, the average investor, greater flexibility by having two more options to choose from, a proven method of determining when stocks are not the best choice for beating the Dow, and where to invest in the coming year to achieve the most reward with least amount of risk. Worrying about the prospect of a stock market decline is now a thing of the past because you'll always keep winning—in any market.

The key to the remarkable results I've shown this method can achieve is the discipline to put the same investment to the same test with as little as a half hour of research year after year, selling those investments that fail to measure up, and buying those that do.

It's a method that boils down to just a few straightforward steps and the use of some common sense. When it comes to making money: buy cheap, sell dear; work smarter, not harder; and *keep it simple*. Always.

BIBLIOGRAPHY

Periodicals

Abelson, Alan. "Long Hot Summer." *Barron's*, February 23, 1998: 1.

Flickinger, Barbara, and Katherine McManus. "Bankruptcy Aftershocks: Have Public Finance Foundations Been Shaken?" *Public Management* 78, no. 1: 16–25.

Galbraith, John Kenneth. "The 29th Parallel." *Atlantic*, January 1987: 62–66.

Kadlec, Daniel. "The Dow Dogs Won't Hunt." *Time*, December 8, 1997: 76.

———. "Bonds Away! Stocks May Not Be the Place to Play." *Time*, January 19, 1998: 48.

Laderman, Jeffrey M. "Don't Worry, Be Bullish." *Business Week*, August 4, 1997: 28–29.

Leland, John. "Blessed by the Bull." *Newsweek*, April 27, 1998: 5–53.

Newsweek. "Big Mac for the Big Apple: Municipal Assistance Corporation." June 23, 1975: 29.

O'Higgins, Michael. "New Winning Strategy from the Inventor of *The Dogs of the Dow*." *Bottom Line*, April 15, 1998: 5–6.

Palette, Mark. "Most Californians Back Bail-out of Orange County." *Los Angeles Times* 114, March 11, 1995: A1.

Pauley, David, with Gretchen Browne. "Grant's Great Collapse." *Newsweek*, October 13, 1975: 81.

Samuelson, Robert J. "Bankrupt NY: No Funds for Fun City." *New Republic*, May 10, 1975: 17–19.

————. "Why We're Married to the Market." *Newsweek*, April 27, 1998: 47–50.

Sloan, Allen. "This Can Go On (Oh, No It Can't)." *Newsweek*, April 27, 1998: 54, 56–57.

Time. "Big Apple on the Brink." April 7, 1975: 50–51.

————. "Now Everyone Is Really Scared." October 13, 1975: 20.

————. "Grant Goes Under." October 13, 1975: 64.

Books

Arbel, Avner. *How to Beat the Market with High-Performance Generic Stocks*. New York: New American Library, 1986.

Blamer, Thomas, and Richard Schulman. *Dow Three Thousand: The Investment Opportunity of the 1980s*. New York: Simon & Schuster, 1982.

Brown, David L., and Kassandra Bentley. *Wall Street City: Your Guide to Investing on the Web*. New York: John Wiley & Sons, 1997.

Bruck, Connie. *The Predators' Ball: The Inside Story of Drexel Burnham and the Rise of the Junk Bond Raiders*. New York: Penguin Books, 1989.

Burrough, Bryan, and John Helyar. *Barbarians at the Gate: The Fall of RJR Nabisco*. New York: HarperCollins, 1991.

Cobleigh, Ira U. *Happiness Is a Stock That Lets You Sleep at Night*. New York: Donald I. Fine, 1989.

Downes, John, and Jordan Elliot Goodman. *Dictionary of Finance and Investment Terms*. 3rd ed. Happauge, N.Y.: Barron's Educational Series, 1991.

Fabozzi, Frank J. *Bond Markets, Analysis, and Strategies*, 3rd ed. New York: Prentice-Hall, 1995.

Farrell, Paul B. *Expert Investing on the Net: Making More Money Online*. New York: John Wiley & Sons, 1996.

Fisher, Kenneth. *Super Stocks*. Homewood, IL.: Dow Jones-Irwin, 1984.

Hoover, Gary, Alta Campbell, and Patrick J. Spain, editors. *Hoover's*

Handbook of American Business. Austin, TX: The Reference Press, 1995.

Investor's Business Daily Guide to the Markets. New York: John Wiley & Sons, 1996.

Johnson, Haynes B. *Sleepwalking Through*. New York: Anchor Books, 1992.

Kaufman, Phyllis C., and Arnold Corrigan. *How to Choose a Discount Broker*. Stamford, CT.: Longmeadow Press, 1987.

Lynch, Peter, with John Rothchild. *One Up on Wall Street*. New York: Simon & Schuster, 1989.

Malkiel, Burton G. *A Random Walk Down Wall Street*. New York: W.W. Norton & Company, 1990.

Mattera, Philip. *Inside U.S. Business: A Concise Encyclopedia of Leading Industries*. Homewood, IL: Dow Jones-Irwin, 1987.

O'Higgins, Michael, with John Downes. *Beating the Dow*. New York: HarperCollins, 1991.

O'Neil, William J. *How to Make Money in Stocks: A Winning System in Good Times or Bad*. New York: McGraw-Hill, 1988.

Renberg, Werner. *All About Bond Funds: A Complete Guide for Today's Investors*. New York: John Wiley & Sons, 1995.

Rolo, Charles J., and Robert J. Klein. *Gaining on the Market: Your Complete Guide to Investment Strategy*. Rev. ed. Boston: Little, Brown & Company, 1988.

Sann, Paul. *The Lawless Decade*. New York: Crown Publishers, 1957.

Sindell, Kathleen. *Investing Online for Dummies*. Foster City, CA: IDG Books Worldwide, Inc., 1998.

Stillman, Richard J. *Dow Jones Industrial Average: History and Role in an Investment Strategy*. Homewood, IL.: Dow Jones-Irwin, 1987.

Walden, Gene. *The 100 Best Stocks to Own in America*. Chicago: Longman Financial Services Publishing, 1989.

Weiss, Geraldine, and Janet Lowe. *Dividends Don't Lie: Finding Value in Blue Chip Stocks*. Chicago: Longman Financial Services Publishing, 1988.

Zipf, Robert. *How the Bond Market Works*. 2nd ed. New York: New York Institute of Finance, 1997.

Zweig, Martin E. *Winning on Wall Street*. New York: Warner Books, 1986.

INDEX

Page numbers of illustrations, charts, and graphics appear in italics.

ABOUT THE AUTHORS

Michael B. O'Higgins is the CEO of his own money management firm, O'Higgins Asset Management Inc., based in Miami, Florida, recently ranked the number one top new fund by *Smart Money* magazine and number five by the *Wall Street Journal*. Leading investment performance measurement firms place him in the top 10 percent of all money managers in the United States.

His unusual approach to managing money has been the subject of articles in the *Wall Street Journal*, the *New York Times*, *Forbes*, the *Financial Times*, *USA Today*, *Financial World*, *Money*, *Business Week*, and *Barron's*.

He has also appeared as a special guest on PBS's *Wall $treet Week*, CNBC's *Smart Money*, and CNNfn.

In 1990, he completed work on *Beating the Dow* (Harper-Collins, 1991), a top-selling investment book on how nonprofessionals can outperform most money managers using the thirty components of the Dow Jones Industrial Average. His book has been critically acclaimed by investment experts around the world and has enabled hundreds of thousands of small investors to achieve stellar investment returns since its publication.

He was born in San Tomé, Venezuela, in 1947. His father was employed in the petroleum industry, and he grew up living and studying in various countries in South America, Southeast Asia, North Africa, and Europe before returning to the United States in 1965.

After earning a B.S. in economics from Siena College in Albany, New York, in 1970 and working briefly for New York State, then the Procter & Gamble company, he entered the investment business in 1971 as a stockbroker trainee for Spencer Trask & Company, working there, and later at White, Weld & Company, until he decided to start his own money management firm in 1978.

He is married with four children, an avid tennis player, and enjoys (but hopes to lower) a 23 handicap in golf.

John McCarty is a novelist, television writer, and the author of more than twenty nonfiction books covering a variety of subjects, notably the film and broadcast media. His collaborative efforts include books on selling strategies, human resource management, and professional organizing techniques.

He was born in Albany, New York, in 1944. After graduating from high school in 1962, he attended Boston University, where he majored in communications (broadcasting and film). Following a stint in the Peace Corps, where he worked as an educational television volunteer in Bogotá, Colombia, he returned to the States and worked in broadcasting for a number of years, then became an advertising copywriter for General Electric Company. He left that in 1983 to become a full-time author.

He is married with two children and five cats, an avid follower of professional golf, and a player himself with an 18 handicap.

For additional information contact:

The O'Higgins Asset Management, Inc.
Web site: www.ohiggins.com

Or

Beating the Dow with Bonds
P.O. Box 547294
Surfside, FL 33154
Phone: 305-861-3218
Fax: 305-861-9852
E-mail: BTDWB@ohiggins.com